OMANI PR(

is a collection of popular sayings
doctor, political agent and traveller
century.

Ibrahim an-Nazzam defined the qualities of the best proverbs as brevity, good sense, a beautiful metaphor, and a fine simile. Al-Maidani, whose anthology made in the fifth century A.H. is cited by Jayakar as F.A.P. (Freytag's edition of Maidani's *Arabum Proverbia*) assures us that most classical Arabic proverbs arose from some historical incident, since forgotten. Others derive from al-Quran al-Karim, literary masterpieces, fables, and riddles. A number possess neat equivalents in English, here printed beside their literal English translations.

Proverbs are a key to a nation's psychology, its political, religious and social ideals, and such preoccupations as weather, neighbours, and animals. The very internal contradictions shown by two proverbs (like 'too many cooks spoil the broth' and 'many hands make light work') indicate the complexity of a mental world coping with a sequence of invasions and drought, famine, or pestilence. The present stability and prosperity of the Sultanate of Oman contrasts with the uncertainties prevalent a century ago, when *Omani Proverbs* was compiled.

A. S. G. JAYAKAR, Agency Surgeon at Muscat, officiated also as Political Agent many times. The rare Arabian *tahr* (a mountain goat named *Hemitragus jayakari* after him) is now protected in a special nature reserve in Oman. Jayakar's long-term interest in his adopted Oman is worthily commemorated by this first reprint of his original collection.

OMANI
PROVERBS

A.S.G. JAYAKAR

THE OLEANDER PRESS

The Oleander Press
17 Stansgate Avenue
Cambridge CB2 2QZ
England

The Oleander Press
210 Fifth Avenue
New York, N.Y. 10010
U.S.A.

British Library Cataloguing in Publication Data

Omani proverbs. – (Arabia past and present;
v. 20)
1. Proverbs, Arabic
I. Jayakar, A. S. G.   II. Series
398'.9'927   PN6519.A7

ISBN 0-906672-12-0

Sponsored by Muna Noor Incorporated, and
reprinted with slight amendments
from the *Journal* of the Bombay Branch
of the Royal Asiatic Society, volume 21, 1900–3.
The photograph of A. S. G. Jayakar is reproduced
by courtesy of H.B.M. Ambassador, Muscat, Oman.

Printed and bound in Great Britain

Foreword

Omani Proverbs is a collection of popular sayings compiled at the end of the nineteenth century by Surgeon Lt. Col. A. S. G. Jayakar, Agency Surgeon in Muscat from 1870 to 1900, who travelled widely in Oman, and contributed to learned journals studies on the Omani and Shheri dialects of Arabic. The rare Arabian *tahr* or mountain goat is named Hemitragus *jayakari* after him.

Ibrahim an-Nazzam defined the qualities of the best proverbs as brevity, good sense, a beautiful metaphor, and a fine simile. Al-Maidani, whose anthology of the fifth century A.H. is cited throughout by Jayakar as F.A.P. (Freytag's *Arabum Proverbia* collected by Maidani), assures us that most classical Arabic proverbs were occasioned by some historical incident, now forgotten. Others derive from the Quran, literary masterpieces, fables, or riddles. A number correspond to English equivalents, here printed beside literal English translations.

Proverbs are one key to a nation's psychology, and its political, religious and social ideals, and even such preoccupations as neighbours, the weather, or animals. Contradictory proverbs such as 'Too many cooks spoil the broth' and 'Many hands make light work' indicate the complexity of a mental world attempting to cope with foreign invasions and domestic crises such as civil strife, drought, or famine. The present stability and prosperity of the Sultanate of Oman contrasts strikingly with the uncertainties prevalent while Jayakar was collecting these proverbs a hundred years ago. His long-term interest in his adopted Oman is commemorated by this first reprint of his painstaking compilation.

Atmaram Sadashiva Grandin Jayakar was born in Bombay on 23 October 1844, and at the age of 15 married Dwarkabai Putoba, a lady then aged 12. He studied medicine at the Grant Medical College from 1862 to 1867, and in July 1867 obtained a licence to practise medicine and surgery from the Royal College of Physicians in London and a licence to practise surgery from the Royal College of Surgeons in London.

He passed the competitive examination of the Indian Medical Service on 12 August 1867, and at the Army Medical School, Royal Victoria Hospital, Netley (1 October 1867 to 8 February 1868), he passed the examination eighth out of twelve.

Jayakar sailed to India on the *Serapis*, leaving on 14 March 1868 and arriving on 16 April, first as Assistant Surgeon successively in the Presidency, North Division, Bombay, Northern District, and eventually Muscat, which he reached in January 1873. Originally appointed Civil Surgeon, he was absent on sick leave from July 1874 to May 1875. Shortly thereafter he produced a useful article, 'The medical topography of Muscat', which appeared in the 1876–7 *Administration Reports of the Persian Gulf Political Residency and Muscat Political Agency*, reprinted complete in ten volumes by Archive Editions (1986). Jayakar is first noted as Surgeon-Major in 1880, acting as Political Agent in place of Major Grant for most of July. In 1881, he attended Sultan Turki ibn Sa'id between 2 and 7 November, and performed the same service during the Sultan's fever in February 1884. The first mention of his appointment to Lieutenant-Colonel occurs in 1891–92, both before and after which he was continually called upon to act as Political Agent during periods when the Agent himself went on leave, retiring on 2 May 1900, after nearly thirty years in Muscat.

Atmaram Jayakar's was the first-ever collection of *Omani Proverbs*, and has since been translated for the Ministry of National Heritage and Culture by Muhammad Amin 'Abdullah as *Al-'Umaniyyun; hikmuhum wa amthaluhum ash-sha'biyyah*. Coincidentally, and after the present reprint was planned, the Sultan's School at Seeb has produced a new compilation entitled *Al-amthal ash-sha'biyyah fi Sultanat 'Uman*, adding a large number of proverbs previously unrecorded, and Khalifah bin 'Abdullah bin Salim al-Humaidi of Ruwi has published the first volume of his *Aqwal 'Uman li kull az-zaman* (1986) on popular sayings. The continuing importance and individuality of the Omani proverb is thus amply demonstrated, from the nineteenth century through to the twentieth. Popular wisdom and common sense have been enshrined in these sayings, which deserve to be made available again for another generation in the year that sees the culmination of the Omani educational system in the establishment of the University. The publishers gratefully acknowledge the book's sponsorship by Muna Noor Incorporated, Muscat, Sultanate of Oman.

THE OLEANDER PRESS

1986

OMANI PROVERBS

A study of the proverbs and maxims of a nation is as essential to the philologist, to whom they are invaluable as a storehouse of the dialectical and linguistic peculiarities exhibited in the expression of thoughts, while yet the nation was only in an early condition of civilization, as to the philosopher who can often trace in them the inner springs of human action. No description or picture can convey more forcibly to the mind the habits, manners, and the general mode of thought of a particular people than an insight into their proverbs, which are mostly couched in the familiar words and thoughts of ordinary daily life.

One of the greatest peculiarities of the Arabic language is the concise and compact mode in which thoughts, often of a complicated nature, can be expressed. This peculiarity and the character of the people as a highly observant race, have combined to produce a proverbial literature unsurpassed in any other language and deserving of a careful study. Scattered and separated in some instances by almost impassable barriers as the modern Arabs are, they can hardly at present be considered a united nation ; their habits, their occupations, their aspirations, and even their modes of thought, all more or less modified and influenced by the circumstances and conditions of life in which they live in each separate district, have acquired such distinctive features as to give rise not only to a dialect, but also to maxims and proverbs peculiar to each community.

The physical features and geographical position of the province of ' Omán have isolated its inhabitants for centuries from the rest of the Arabs, which renders a study of their dialect and proverbs of special interest. When we look at the immense sandy desert which borders it on the north and west, and which has hitherto almost effectually cut off all land communication with the rest of the country, we cannot fail to wonder at the manner in which the ' Ománees have still retained one of the great racial peculiarities, namely, that of expressing ideas and thoughts in the shape of proverbs—a mode which undoubtedly possesses the double advantage of conciseness and impressiveness. Whether we hear them in the palace or in the shop, in the field or on the roadside, they are the same homely ungarnished truths, expressed in the fewest and simplest possible words, and brought more or less forcibly to the minds of both the speaker and the hearer by the context of the subject of conversation. Even a casual observer cannot help noticing the extensive use the 'Ománees make of proverbial sayings in their conversation, and admiring the facility with which they adapt them to the circumstances calling for their use.

As a rule the 'Ománees may be considered to be a peace-loving and law-abiding people, and although almost every man carries arms of some kind or another, nothing would induce him to use them unless driven to an extremity. They have a great aversion to fighting, and all possible means for an amicable settlement of a dispute are sought and tried before any recourse to arms is had.

Barring in maritime places, the general avocation of the Hadr (inhabitants of towns and villages) of ' Omán is that of an agricultural nature. The date-palm and the camel principally engross their attention and enter conspicuously into their proverbial similes. Individual wealth or property (مال), which has come to be synonymous with date-palms, is gauged by the number of the trees possessed, whilst tribal wealth or strength is judged by the number of camels which a tribe can muster in times of exigency. The loss of either is therefore looked upon as a calamity.

A superstitious belief in the existence and power of supernatural beings forms also an essential feature of the 'Ománee character, as may be seen in Nos. 132 and 200, whilst a belief in sorcery or magic (*vide* No. 230), especially in its capability of transforming human beings into lower animals, has gained even a stronger hold on the minds of the people. It is not to be wondered at, that under the strong influence of such beliefs, disease is frequently attributed to the agency of the evil spirit, and death often looked upon as only a transformation of form. The enchanter or sorcerer being a destroyer of human peace and happiness is considered a tyrant (No. 229) and universally dreaded ; extreme care is therefore taken not to offend persons who have the reputation of being expert in the Black Art. This fear even extends to the animals which are supposed to be in the special service of the enchanters, for instance, the hyena, which is considered to be employed for riding upon, and the lapwing, which acts as their messenger (No. 230).

Blood feuds and consequent blood revenge, which have from time
immemorial formed an important part of Arab life, have acquired in
'Omán even a greater importance and have become a fruitful source of
inter-tribal troubles. The Hináwees, the descendants of the immigrants
from Yaman, and the Gafrees, the descendants of the immigrants from
the north, under one or other of which great political factions the
tribes of ' Omán are grouped, bear perpetual enmity towards each other,
and under the present system in which personal grievances are often
looked upon as tribal affairs, causes constantly arise to foment and
keep up this bitter feeling of hatred between the two great divisions.
In this manner murder and pillage, however personal in their nature,
have to be avenged sooner or later by the tribe of the victim against
the tribe to which the culprit belongs, so that the punishment more
often than otherwise falls on an innocent person (*vide* No. 256).

Another feature which will strike the reader as remarkable in the
following paper is the great dependence the people of ' Omán place on
luck (*vide* No. 36). It is not, however, to be inferred that they are
absolutely lazy ; on the contrary, they are an active race, but their
exertions are generally limited to grooves to which they have been
accustomed for centuries, and to an extent which sometimes falls short
of success. Nature has undoubtedly helped to spoil the ' Ománee in
this respect, by having furnished him in the date-palm with ready
means of sustenance and protection from the inclemency of the weather, and thus exempting him from the toil and labour so inseparable
from agricultural life in other countries. The date-palm, which is the
principal object of his care and attention, exacts from him service
which costs him hardly any labour, whilst the camel, his principal
means of locomotion, frequently depends upon its own resources for its
food.

Credulity plays an important part in the social and religious life of
the people of ' Omán, who while exhibiting this sign of weak-minded-
ness retain nevertheless the great national character of the Arab race—
of being unimaginative and practical. Their almost universal belief
in the supernatural and fabulous, as illustrated in the following paper,
is a fair indication of their credulous nature, whilst proverb No. 241
illustrates not only their gullibility, but also a character, examples of
which are not infrequently met with in the East.

Upon the whole, however, the moral principles inculcated in the
proverbs and aphorisms of the ' Ománees are sound, and may be considered the heritage of mankind in general from remote ages. It will be
seen how closely some of the proverbs given here resemble in their
application those of other nations, though the mode of thought and

expression must necessarily be strikingly different. The simple homely truths which underlie all proverbial literature, and which have been discovered as a result of experience of ages, are universally the same, whatever the mode of expression may be.

In order to enable the reader to recognize the peculiarities of the 'Ománee dialect, the mode of spelling adopted throughout the following pages is such as would convey easily to his mind the phonetic differences between the standard and 'Ománee Arabic. With this view all the important vowel marks are shown, and no attempt has been made either to correct the orthography or to assimilate it to that of the standard Arabic. In many instances a striking resemblance to common and well-known English proverbs in their application is observed, and in such cases English equivalents are given. In a few instances the proverbs seem to have come from classical Arabic proverbs, or to have a great resemblance to Arabic proverbs current in Egypt, in which cases a reference is given to the books in which they may be found.

In the following pages the following abbreviations are used :—

B. A. P. *for* Burckhardt's Arabic Proverbs.

Eng. eq. *for* English equivalent.

F. A. P. *for* Freytag's *Arabum Proverbia*.

Lit. *for* literally.

' Om. *for* ' Ománee.

مَاۡتَاۡيِ يَضۡرِبُو عَلَيۡه قَامۡ يَرۡعَى   I

He (a bull) is brought for leaping but keeps on grazing.

Applied to a person who has an important undertaking before him, but engages in some trivial affair.

مَاۡتَاۡيِ 'Om. measure of past part. of اۡتَى]=*he came.* قَامۡ ' Om. for قَامۡ]=*he commenced, he remained.*

أَخَذۡتَ أَحَسَانَكَ بِلِسَانَكَ   2

You have taken away (the beauty of) your kindness by your tongue (unkind words).

Eng. eq. A gift with a kind countenance is a double gift.

اِذَا بَرَلَكَ ٱلۡقَمَرُ لَا تَبَالِي فِي ٱلنُّجُومُ   3

If the moon shines for you, do not mind the stars.

If one has the support of a great person, he can afford to be independent of his subordinates or others inferior to him in rank.

The modern Egyptians have a similar proverb. Conf. B. A. P. No. 4.

$$\text{اِذَا جَارَ عَلَيْكَ الزَّمَانُ جُورُ عَلَى الاَرْضِ} \quad 4$$

If fortune (time) oppresses you, oppress land.

This is an exhortation for exertion in hard times.

$$\text{اِذَا سَاحَ النَّبَاتُ حَيْثُ يَأَدِّيكَ اللَّيْلُ بَاتُ} \quad 5$$

When the operation of fecundating the date-palms with the pollen of the male palms is over, sleep wherever the night overtakes you. *Lit.* When the pollen is all gone.

It is the time when the real cold weather is supposed to be over in ' Omán.

نَبَاتُ ' Om. = the germinating principle or pollen obtained from the flowers of the male date-palm.

$$\text{اِذَا كَانَ المُتَكَلِّم مَجْنُون يَكُون المُسْتَمِع عَاقِل} \quad 6$$

If the speaker is mad, the hearer should be wise.

It shows the necessity of caution on the part of a hearer in believing what he is informed and in acting upon it.

Eng. eq. Believe not all you hear, and report not all you believe.

$$\text{اِذَا مَا جَادَت الرَّوبَة مَا تَجُود الصَّلَالَة} \quad 7$$

If the curdled milk is not good, its water is (also) not good.

If there is no good in the principal person of a house or tribe, one must not expect to find it in a person in an inferior position.

الصَّلَالَة = the water which separates from milk on churning it, or on boiling new milk.

$$\text{اِذَا مَاتَت جَاعِدَة فِي مَكْرَان مَا يَغْلَى السَّمَن فِي عُمَان} \quad 8$$

If a ewe dies in Makrán, *ghee* (clarified butter) won't become dear in ' Omán.

Applied to trivial events or circumstances not likely to have even a remote effect.

Eng. eq. Two swallows do not make a summer. جَاعِدَة 'Om. = a ewe.

٩ اِذَا مَا سَدّ عَضْقَها وَلَّا مِن عَرْقِيَّا

If its (date-palm's) produce is not enough, have it out of its roots.

On the advisability of uprooting or selling off a thing which entails profitless labour. It is also applied to persons.

عَضِمَة 'Om. = a cluster of dates on the stalk. وَلَّ stands for اِلَّا.

١٠ اِذَا مَا طَاعَكَ الدَّهْر طِيعَهُ حَتَّى تَكُون زِبِيعَه

If fortune does not obey you, follow it so that you may become its companion.

Adapt yourself to the times.

Eng. eq. As the year is, so must your pot seethe.

There is a similar proverb in classical Arabic. Conf. F. A. P., Tom III, No. 2965.

١١ سِم شَايِع و البَطْن جَايِع

(His) name is renowned, but his stomach is hungry.

Applied to one who has a big name but is penniless; also to a vain boaster.

The form جَايِع (*hungry*) is rarely used, but is employed here evidently for rhyming, the commoner forms being جَوْعَان and جِيعَان. سِم stands for اِسْم

Eng. eq. Empty vessels make the greatest sound.

There is a similar proverb in classical Arabic. Conf. F. A. P., Caput XXVI, No. 132.

١٢ تُوكِل مَال الزَّوج وِتَحِنّ لِلمُطَلَّق

She lives at the expense (*lit.* eats the property) of the present husband, but sings the praises (*lit.* yearns towards) of the one that has divorced her.

Applied to an ungrateful person.

كِلْ مِنْ بَصَلْ عَمَ يَحَصَلْ 13

Eat of an onion whatever (portion) you may get.

Partake of a good thing even if it be a little, onions like radishes being considered by the people of 'Omán a delicacy.

A good thing even if it be a little is not to be despised.

كِلْ مِنْ ثُوم بِمَا تُرِزِم 14

Eat of garlic as much as you can.

One cannot have too much of a good thing. تُرِزِم from 'Om. رِأم =he was able.

كِلْ مِنْ زُويِد وَلَوْ عُويِد 15

Eat of a radish even if it be a leaflet.

If one cannot get the whole of a good thing, even a small part of it ought to be accepted. زُريِد 'Om. =a radish.

كَلْنَا مِنْشِ يَ سِيعَانَّ وَعَتيْنَا شِ وَرَأَ العَلَّة 16

We have eaten (dates) out of you. O basket, and thrown you behind the house.

Said of an ungrateful person.

سِيعَانَّ =a small basket made of green palm leaves. عَتَى 'Om. =he threw away. عَلَّة 'Om. =a house, originally a pen to hold camels.

إِلا فَتَكَ اللَّحِم شَرِب المَرَقَ 17

If you lose the meat, drink the gravy.

Eng. eg. Half a loaf is better than no bread. Conf. B. A. P., No. 662.

إلّ stands for إذا.

اَلِّي يَلُمّ الحَوُل وِيَذْرِى بَهْ لابِد مِنْ طَشْ الرَّهَمْ يَصِيبَه 18

This is a Badawee proverb. He who gathers weeds and takes shelter under them, will necessarily get wet directly it rains.

Eng. eq. Do not lean on a broken reed.

الجُوَل ' Om. = weeds, rubbish. أَيِّ stands for الَّذِي.

أَمَّا جِلِس وِهِجِع وَأَمَّا ضَرَب وَوَجَع   19

Either sit and remain listless, or strike and cause pain.

Either never attempt or accomplish. This is somewhat similar to
the Syriac proverb, اذا ضربت اوجع واذا طعمت اشبع (Burton).
Conf. also F. A. P., Caput I, No. 103.

أَمَّا طَاهِر يَصَلَّا بَه وَأَمَّا رِجِس يِرمَا بَه   20

It (a prayer-mat) is either clean enough to pray upon or unclean
enough to be thrown away.

Applied to a thing or case to which there are only two extremes without any mean between.

أَمَّا فْتَم بَّبَك وِتَجَمَل وِلَا شَدَه وِتْخَمَل   21

Either open your door and do good (to others), or close it and become
unknown.

أَمَّا وَأَمَّا وَأَمَّا   22

Either, or, or. One of the three things must happen to overcome the
difficulty.

It is related that a certain wazeer having a spite against a certain
man whom he wished to be killed, told the king whose wazeer he was,
that a certain horse which he had received as a present knew to speak,
and that there was only one man in his kingdom who could under-
stand the language. The man, who was the wazeer's enemy, was
immediately brought before the king, but as he persistently denied
having any knowledge of the horse-language, his head was ordered
to be struck off. He was, however, allowed a respite of three days
in order to make up his mind, whether he would talk with the horse
or lose his life, and ordered to be kept with the horse in the same
stable. The man was lost in thinking how to get over the difficulty,
and kept constantly saying, أَمَّا وَأَمَّا وَأَمَّا (*either, or, or*), which the
horseman reported to the king. He therefore sent for him and asked

him the meaning of his words. The man again declared his inability
to talk with the horse, and pardon having been promised him, he said
that he was thinking, that one of the three things must happen for him
to get over the difficulty, namely, that either he should die, or the sultan,

or the horse (اَمَّا اَنَا اَمُوت وَ اَمَّا السُّلْطَان وَ اَمَّا الفُرَّس). The king
having thus found out, that that was only a plot against the poor man's
life designed by the wazeer, ordered the latter to be killed instead.

23 اَنَا سَكَبْت المَأْى عَلَى غِي السِّرَا لَا اَنَا بِالمَأْى وَلَا اَنَا بِغِي السِّرَا

I threw away the water on account of (seeing) the mirage, but here
I am without any water and without the mirage.

Applied to one who gives up a reality for a shadow, and loses both
in consequence of it. غِي السِّرَا ' Om. = mirage.

24 اَنَا شَايِف خَيْر وَخُضْرَة مَا اَسْتَعْجِب مِن جَرَاد المَقْبَرَة

I have seen plenty and prosperity (*lit.* green), and am therefore not
filled with wonder at the sight of *jarád-ul-mukubreh* (*lit.* a locust of the
grave-yard).

Said of a person who has seen better times. *Jarád-ul-mukubreh* is the
name technically applied to an orthopterous insect commonly found
near grave-yards.

25 اَنَا شَايِف مَسْكَد وَكِيتَانَهَا مَا اَسْتَعْجِب مِن دَارْسِيت وَكِيزَانَهَا

I have seen Maskad (Maskat) and its forts, and am not therefore
filled with wonder at the sight of Darseit and its earthen ewers.

The people of ' Omán spell the name of the town of Maskat as Maskad.
In former days there used to be many potteries at Darseit near Matrah.

كُوت *pl.* كِيتَان ' Om. = fort—from Hindustanee كُوت

كُوز *p.* كِيزَان ' Om. = an earthen ewer.

26 اَنَا مَا شَايِف دَم فِي الخِتَانَة وَالقَيْض فِي شَرْجِبَانَة

I have not seen the blood (only) of circumcision and the *kaid* (only) of *sharjabáneh.*

Said in self-praise.

اَلْبِيْضٍ | stands for اَلْقَيْظ = Summer, the season of dates, when the people visit the date plantations and enjoy themselves generally.

شَرْجِبَان = *Solanum violaceum* ; it grows wild in ʻOmán.

27   أَنَا أَقُولْ جَمَلْ و أَنْتَ تَقُولْ جَبَلْ

I say " a camel," and you say " a mountain."

This proverb is used when there is a great difference of opinion, or when an answer to a question relates to something totally different from what the question is about.

28   أَنَ أَقُولْ طَابِقْ وَأَنْتَ تَقُولْ طَالِقْ

I say "joined," and you say " separated."

Applied in the same sense as the last proverb.

29   إِن بَغِيتْ تَجِيدْ انْظُرْ بِمَا فِي كَفَّكْ و إِن بَغِيتْ تَلِيشْ انْظُرْ

بِاللَّذِي يَقْفِيكْ

If you wish to be generous, see (first) what is in your hand ; and if you wish to fight, see (first) who will follow you.

On the advisability of seeing first what one's means are before undertaking a thing.

Eng. eq. Look before you leap.

تَلِيشْ from لَاشْ in the sense of plundering or laying waste a country.

30   إِن رَأَيتْ صَاحِبَكْ عَسَلْ لَا تَلْحَسُهُ كُلَّهُ

If you find your friend to be honey, do not lick him altogether.

On the advisability of not killing the goose with golden eggs.

31   إِن كَان نِيَّتَكْ عَمَارْ مَا يَضُرَّكْ ضَرِيطْ الْحَمَارْ

If your motive is good, an ass' breaking wind will not injure you.

Let not little things interfere with the carrying out of your purpose, if your motive is good.

$$ \text{32} \qquad \text{أَيْ وَالعَزَّتَيْنِ مَا يَنْفَعْ} $$

Repentance is of no avail.

Eng. eq. No use crying over spilt milk.

أَيْ وَالعَزَّتَيْنِ is a common phrase for expressing regret at the loss of an opportunity, or any other reason for repentance,

$$ \text{33} \qquad \text{بَاذَرِ سِدِّ سِيْنِ وَ مِدْيَنِ أَجْرِيَيْنِ} $$

He has sown only two *sidis* (of seed) when he has borrowed two *jarees.*

Applied to a person who borrows more than he would be able to return, in consequence of his utilizing only a very small portion of the loan.

Sidis = an 'Ománee dry measure equal to a Bombay *páti.* *Jaree* = 30 *sidis* or *pátis.*

$$ \text{34} \qquad \text{الْبُجِمَّة أَزْوَجْ مِنِ الثَّلْعَة} $$

A bruise is lighter (to bear) than a laceration.

A broken arm is better than a broken head.

بُجِمَّة 'Om. = a tumour due to a contusion.

$$ \text{35} \qquad \text{الْبُخْت اِلَا جَادْ قَالُوا صَاحِبُهْ أُسْتَاد وَ الْبُخْت اِلَا بَارْ قَالُوا} $$
$$ \text{صَاحِبُهْ عِيَّارْ} $$

When fortune is propitious, they say the possessor of it is a master (in the art), but when fortune is adverse, they say the possessor of it is a cheat.

Eng. eq. He dances well to whom fortune pipes.

$$ \text{36} \qquad \text{بِالْمَرْزَقْ لَا بِالْمَحْدَقْ} $$

By means of good fortune, and not by means of cleverness.

Wealth is not acquired by being clever but by having a good fortune.

$$ برقا قضاك لا اَستَخِيلُك وان اِسْتَخِلتَ لا تَتَّبِع عليه \quad 37 $$

Do not think of lightning behind you, but if you think and prognosticate rain do not go in that direction.

Against paying any attention to backbiters or taking any measures against them.

$$ بُرمَة الشِرك ما تَثُور \quad 38 $$

A pot in partnership does not boil.

Eng. eq. A pot that belongs to many is ill stirred and worse boiled.

بُرمَة ' Om. = an earthen cooking pot. ثار ' Om. for فَار = it boiled.

$$ بعرَه يَكِس في دَبرَه سماذ د في اَرضُه \quad 39 $$

Its (the donkey's) dung is sprinkled over its own ulcer ; the bullock's manure is in its own pasture land.

Applied to one who wastes nothing, or as in the proverb, utilizes the dung of his animals for their own purposes.

The dried dung of donkeys is often pounded and dusted over their galled backs as a remedy in ' Omán.

$$ تَبغى تَزعَل ما مَتَفِيَّة من شغلان بيتها \quad 40 $$

She wants to be angry, but is not free from her household duties.

Applied to a person who wants to undertake a profitless task, when his or her hands are already full of more important matters.

زَعَل ' Om. = he became angry; زَعلان = angry. مَتَفِيَّة ' Om. = at leisure, free. شَغلان ' Om. *pl.* of شُغَل work, business.

$$ تَبغى من تِبنُها واَعنابُها وحاتَم على بابها \quad 41 $$

You want figs and grapes out of it (the garden), whilst Hátim is at its gate (as gardener in charge). It would be impossible for one to have the product of a garden whilst a liberal man like Hátim is in charge of it.

Applied in the sense of two incompatible things or two opposite elements not being able to exist together.

$$ بَكَّايَة وِمَّيِت بْلَيْا 42 $$

A professional crier and her son is dead.

Applied to a person who meets with circumstances favourable to his or her design.

In every village and town in ' Omán there are certain women who, though not paid for their trouble, visit the houses of mourning to help the women there in crying loudly.

$$ بِمَا يَبِيع الأَمَّ مِخَلَّص 43 $$

A thief can afford to sell (a stolen thing) at whatever price he may do so. He incurs no loss.

Said of a person who parts with a thing easily after having obtained it without any trouble or expense.

Lightly come, lightly go.

$$ بِنْت الصَّايِغ تَشْتَهِى الصُّوغ وِبِنْت النَّسَّاج عَرْيَانَة 44 $$

The goldsmith's daughter pines for (lit. desires) ornaments and the weaver's daughter is naked.

Eng. eq. The cobbler's wife is the worst shod.

$$ بِنِي بِالفِضَّة و غَلَّف بِالذَّهَب 45 $$

Build with silver, and cover with gold.

On the advisability of making a good show.

$$ بُو يَاتِى مِن بَطْنَ بِيرَبِّى اغَم بِطَانَه 46 $$

He who begets (a child) from his loins (lit. belly), will rear it whether he wishes or not.

One is bound to defend his own action, or to preserve what he has created, even against his will.

اَغُمْ بَطْنُكَ ' Om.=nolens volens.

$$ 47 \quad بُو يَأَكِل حَلُوَاهَا يَصبُر عَلَى بَلُوَاهَا $$

He who eats her *halwá* must (also) patiently endure her misfortune.
Eng. eq. There is no joy without alloy.

بُو ' Om. for الَّذِى = who, which, &c. Conf. F. A. P., Caput XXIV,
No. 457.

$$ 48 \quad بُو اِمهَا فِي البَيت مَا تَقحَب $$

She whose mother is in the house is not called a whore.

A person who has a good protector is not likely to be abused or
suspected of an evil action.

$$ 49 \quad بُو يَبغِى لَبَنهَا يَبرِق فِي وِجهَا $$

He who wants her (the cow's) milk must look carefully at her face.

On the advisability of examining a thing carefully before buying or
receiving it.

$$ 50 \quad بُو يَجِى اِلَى مَغَارَة يِلَا مَاكَله واَدمَارِه $$

He who comes to the house (*lit.* cave), when he has eaten, causes its
ruin.

Applied in the sense of self-defence and also ingratitude. An enemy
ought to be kept at a distance.

$$ 51 \quad بُو يَجِي مَا مَنهُوم يِجلِس بِلا فَرَاش $$

He who comes uninvited sits (on the bare ground) without a mat.
Eng. eq. Uninvited guests sit on thorns.

$$ 52 \quad بُو يَخجِل مِن بِنت عَمه مَا يَجِيب اَولَاد $$

He who is shy of his wife (*lit.* cousin) does not beget children.
Eng. eq. Faint heart never won fair lady. Conf. B. A. P., No. 620.

بو نخيس نعقتك ما يقصها 53

He whose nose stinks does not cut it off.

On the advisability of using gentle means to reclaim a lost child or friend.

خاس 'Om. = it rotted. نعفة 'Om. = nose.

بو يدور الحال بتييه العلل 54

He who wanders about the town, draws upon himself misfortunes. By misfortunes are here meant diseases, accusations of crime, &c.

On the advisability of not visiting suspicious and dangerous places.

حالل 'Om. pl of حلة = a quarter of a town.

بو يربيها في ثبانه تلدغه في لسانه 55

It (a viper) bites him in the tongue who rears it in the lap.

On ingratitude and returning evil for good.

بو يرضى في جاره تخرب داره 56

He who rejoices over (the misfortunes of) his neighbour will have his house in ruins.

On the advisability of taking a lesson from the misfortunes of others and not rejoicing over them.

بو يزرع الجودات يستدنا الجمايل 57

He who sows generous actions reaps (lit. is rewarded with) good actions.

Eng. eq. The hand that gives gathers.

بو شاقة الشلول كل ما يغلبها موخل 58

A she-camel which carries a whole load is not overcome by (the weight of) a sieve

A person accustomed to undertake great affairs is not likely to be overburdened by a little more responsibility.

مُوْخَل 'Om. for منْخِل = a sieve.

59   بو يشور بعمره ٨ يكسك

He who offers advice of his own accord has to look small.

On the advisability of not offering advice unasked.

بعمره ٨ ' Om. = by himself, of his own accord.

60   بو يصبر ويتآنا ياتى ما يتمنى

He who has patience and waits gets what he desires.

Eng. eq. Everything comes to him who can wait.

61   بو يضرب عمره ٨ ما يبكي

He who beats himself ought not to cry.

One who brings a misfortune upon himself ought not to lament over it.

62   بو في القلوب ما في الدروب

What is in hearts is not (to be said) on the roads.

Secret things must not be talked about excepting in secret places

63   بو بفحها الذيب ما تعدل

A she-goat which has been once attacked by a wolf will never improve.

A tribe which has been once attacked by an enemy does not return to its original prosperous condition owing to the constant dread in which it is.

64   بو بفحم دبة ما يكوره ٨ حبة

He who jumps over a sand-hill will not be caused to tumble by a grain.

He who is in the habit of performing great actions successfully is not likely to fail in doing a small and unimportant thing.

قُحَم ' Om. = he jumped. تَكَفَّر ' Om. = he stumbled.

65   بُو يَلْدَغُهُ الغُول يَهَاب مِن الحَبِل

He who has been (once) bitten by a snake is afraid of (even) a rope.

Experience makes one cautious.

Eng. eq. Burnt child dreads the fire. Once bitten twice shy.

غُول ' Om. = a snake.

66   بُو ما يِدَادَر بِنَفْسه ما يِدَادَ رَبِّه غَيره

What one does not arrange for himself will not be arranged for him by others.

On the advisability of exerting oneself in doing one's own work and not depending upon others for it.

Eng. eq. Never trust to another what you should do yourself.

67   بُو ما يَحمِي دَاره ويُوخَد ثَأره يَكْثُر مَعيَاره

He who does not protect his house and take his revenge increases in blame (*lit.* his blame increases). يُوخَد ' Om. for يَأخَد.

On guarding one's interests and taking revenge when necessary.

68   بُو ما يِزُورْنِي والدِّيَار مُخِيفَة لَا مَرحَبابَه والدِّيَار اَمَان

He who does not visit me when the country is in a state of alarm is not welcome when it is tranquil.

Eng. eq. Peril proves who dearly loves.

69   بُو ما شَايِف اللَّحم يِسْتَعجِب مِن الرِّية

He who has never seen meat is pleased with lungs. Conf. F. A. P., Caput XXIV, No. 474.

70   بُو ما يِعرِفَك ما يِثَمْنَك

He who does not know you, does not value you.

The worth of a thing is only known to those who know it well.

بو ما يَدّ ي في قُفعَتْه ما تَـهمُني صُفعَتْه 71

I am not concerned about his slapping (me) whose bag I have not my hand in.

Eng. eq. A clear conscience fears no accusation. قُفعَة 'Om.=a large bag made of date-palm leaves for bagging dry dates, limes, &c.

البَيْت يُدْخَل مِن بابْه 72

A house is entered by its door.

Applied in the sense of everything having its proper way.

بَيْت طِين ما يَعدَم مِن الطَّحِين 73

A house built of clay cannot be without any flour in it.

It is expected that a great man must possess all ordinary things or good qualities.

A house built of clay means a substantial one in contradistinction to a hut.

بَيْت الظَّالُم خَرَاب 74

The house of a tyrant is a waste (in ruins). Conf. F. A. P., Tom. III, No. 265.

البَيْت كَبِير والرَّبّ خَبِير 75

The house is big, but the Lord knows (what it contains).

A person may appear to be good and great, but his real qualities may not be seen.

Eng. eq A fair face may hide a foul heart.

بَيْضَة اليَوم ولا فَرخ باكُر 76

Rather an egg to-day than a chicken to-morrow.

Eng. eq. One to-day is better than two to-morrow. A bird in the hand is worth two in the bush.

77 بَيْنَ الاَحْبَابِ تَسَاقَطَ الآدَابِ

Among friends ceremonies are not observed (*lit.* are dropped).

Friends need not observe any formalities or ceremonies among themselves.

78 تَرَكِ الذَّنْبِ وِلا تَعَالِجِ تَوْبَةٍ

Leave off sinning and do not try to show repentance.

Prevention is better than cure. Conf. B. A. P., No. 155.

79 التَّوْرِيَان فِدَى السَّكَّرِ

Toriyan is the ransom of sugarcane.

Toriyan is planted in the same field as sugarcane and round about it, so that should any animals or disease attack the field, the *toriyan* may be lost but the sugarcane is saved. The vanguard of an army, which in ' Omán generally consists of slaves or unimportant persons, often saves by its destruction the main body.

تُوْرِيَان ' Om. from H تُوْر = *Cajanus arabicus.*

80 ثُوْرِ بِيدَارِ ضُرْبِ وِ اَزْجَرِ

A gardener's bullock, beat and drive (him).

Applied to a lazy person who cannot be made to work without being constantly urged. بِيدَارِ ' Om. = a gardener. زَجَرِ ' Om. = he drove a bullock in the pit before a well, called the *khabb*, for the purpose of drawing water.

81 الجُرْفِ بُوْمَلُدُوغِ مِنُّه لاَ تَدَخَّل فِيه يَدَكِ ثَانِيَةٍ

Do not put your hand a second time into the hole you have been bitten or stung in before.

On being cautious from past experience.

Eng. eq. Confide not in him who has once deceived you.

82   اَلْبَجَلَب بَعْد العيد

Bringing the goats (to the market) for sale after the ' Eed festival.

Eng. eq. A day after the feast. After death, the doctor.

اَلْبَجَلَب | ' Om. = bringing goats to the market. A few days before the two ' Eed festivals, the people of the villages near Maskat and Matrah bring in their goats for sale in large numbers.

83   جِلْد فَأر ما يَسْتَوِي مِنَّه طَبِل

A drum cannot be made of a rat's skin.

Applied to inappropriateness of things or persons.

Eng. eq. You cannot make a silk purse out of a sow's ear.

84   الجُود بالمَاجُود وكَفّ الخَالِي بِمُو يَجُود

Generosity if there is anything (in the hand), but what is an empty hand to be generous with ? مَاجُود stands for مَوجُود and مُو for مَا.

What is one to be generous with if he has nothing in his hand to give away.

85   جَوعَان فِي الَمَيِضَة وعَطْشَان فِي الشَّرِيعَة

Hungry in a summering place and thirsty in a watering place.

Generally applied to a person who is lazy. During summer or rather the date season, dates are so plentiful in the plantations that even beggars and poor people are allowed to have them as food for the mere trouble of picking them.

Eng. eq. To starve in a cook shop.

86   جِيبُر لَهَا تَيْس مِن هِيل

Bring for her (a she-goat), a ram-goat from Heel.

Applied to a person who is not satisfied with the arguments of the company he is present in, this proverb being employed to express a desire that other and cleverer persons may be called in to satisfy him. *Heel* is the name of a place near Simáil, and Heel goats are remarkable for their power.

87 أَحَاسِبُوا كُلَّ يَوْمٍ تَكُونُوا خُرَا دُومِ

Settle accounts every day that you may be always brothers.

Eng. eq. Short reckonings make long friends. خُرَا stands for
أُخْوَان

88 نَحْسِبُ خُضْرَةً بِلَادٍ وَهِيَ مَقَرْقَاعٍ وَمُجَاجٍ

We believe *Khudreh* to be a town, but it is only (full of) *makurka'a*
and *majaj.*

Applied to a person or thing not answering one's anticipations.

مَقَرْقَاعٍ = *Abutilon tomentosum.* مُجَاجٍ = *Physalis flexuosa.* Both of
them are wild plants common in certain parts.

89 حُسْنُ السُّوقِ زِلاَّ حُسْنُ البِضَاعَةِ

Better to have a good market than good merchandise.

A brisk market would bring in more profit than the mere possession
of superior kinds of goods.

90 حَصَّلَ حَصَلَةَ يَهُودِيٍّ فِي المَسْجِدِ

He fell into the embarrassment of a Jew in a mosque. A Jew would
not know what to do with himself in a mosque.

Eng. eq. Fish out of water.

حَصَلَةَ ' Om. = embarrassment, hence حَصْلاَن ' Om. = confused, embarrassed, the latter word being often applied to a person in a dying
state.

91 مَحْلاَ الحَرْبُ عَلَى المُتَسَقِّرِينَ

Pleasant (sweet) is a war for the peace-makers or lookers on. The
lookers on enjoy the fun of a war without being interested in the issues
of the conflict. تَسَقَّرَ ' Om. = he enjoyed himself.

Eng. eq. Lookers on see more than players.

92 الْحَنْظَلَة مَا تَنْقَلُب جِحَّة

A colocynth gourd can never be transformed into a water-melon
الْحَنْظَلَة stands for الْحَنْظَلَة.

Eng. eq. You cannot wash the blackamoor white.

What is bad in nature can never be transformed into a good thing.

93 الْحِيلَة غَالِبَة القُوّة

Stratagem overcomes strength.

Policy often effects what force cannot.

94 حِيلَة نُصْف مَرْجَلَة

A stratagem is half manliness. Stratagems, which in 'Omán often
mean wily tricks, are lawful for the accomplishment of an object.

95 أَحَابِي حَمَد لَاجَل مُحَمَّد

I salute Hamad for Muhammad's sake.

Eng. eq. Many kiss the child for the nurse's sake.

96 حَيِي مَالَك بِمَال

Revive your property with other property.

If one's property is in a bad state, it is advisable for him to spend
more money on it to restore it to its proper condition.

97 الْخَابُورَة مَخْبُورَة

(The town of) *Kháboreh* is well known.

Applied to a thing which is well known or to any information which
is not new.

Eng. eq. "Queen Anne is dead."

98 خُدُم فِي الشَّمْس وكِل فِي الظَّلّة

Work in the sun and eat in the shade.

Eng. eq. Make hay while the sun shines.

99 خُذ مِن الرَّخِيص نَهَاكَ ومِن الغَالِي عَشَاكَ

Buy (*lit.* take) out of things which are cheap as much as you like, but out of those that are dear just enough for your evening meal.

On the advisability of observing economy.

100 الخَسَارَة مَع بَعْض النَّاس عِيد

The loss (of some) is an occasion for rejoicing (*lit.* 'Eed festival) with others.

The death of the wolf is the life of the lamb.

101 خَلَّفَ لِعَدَاكَ ولَا تَحْتَاج لِحِبَّاكَ

Better to leave it (after death) for your enemies than to want (in your life-time) from your friends.

Eng. eq. Better spare of thine own than ask other men.

102 خُنْفُسَانَة فِي عَيْن أُمَّهَا غَزَالَة

The black beetle *khunfasáneh* in the eyes of its mother is a gazelle.

Every one likes his own production or thing however bad or ugly it may be in the estimation of others. خُنْفُسَانَة ' Om. for خُنْفُسَانَة = *Adesmia cothurnata.* Conf. B. A. P., No. 60.

103 الخَيْر فِي بَطْن الشَّر

Good is (sometimes) produced by (*lit.* inside) evil. What may be considered as a calamity may be productive of good.

Sweet often comes from sour. Conf. F. A. P., Caput I, No. 12.

104 الخَيْل ولَو هَزْلَت مَا يِسَاق عَلَيْهَا السَّمَاد

Manure is not carried on horses, even if they have become lean.

A man with a good origin, however poor he may be, will not condescend to do a mean thing. In 'Omán the task of carrying manure is allotted to donkeys.

105 دَافِع النَّقَم بِاللُّقَم

Ward off anger or punishment by means of a morsel.

On the advisability of paying a bribe or making a present to another person in order to escape the effects of his anger.

106 دَان دَان عَلِي النَّغَالَة

All the drumming for a date of the kind called *nagál*.

This proverb may be employed in two senses : (1) to express that all the fuss that is being made is not for nothing, and (2) to express that so much fuss is being made over only a trifling thing.

Eng. eq. (In the first sense) Where much smoke is there must be some fire. (In the second sense) Great cry and no wool.

دَان دَان 'Om.=a musical party at which women generally hired on festive occasions, such as marriage, &c., sing. نَغَال=the commonest variety of dates in 'Omán.

107 يَدَعِي الحَاصِل ويَتْبَع النَّاصِل

He leaves off what is found and follows what slips off.

He leaves the substance for the shadow.

Eng. eq. Catch not at the shadow, and lose the substance.

108 ذَخَر دَكّ ولا لَكّ

Treasure earth instead of *lacs*.

On the advisability of investing money in land instead of storing it up.

109 يَدَلَّك عَلَى الحَرْب مِن لا يَعِينَك

He shows you the way to war who will not help you.

Persons who are not likely to give any help, or who are not interested, are the very ones most forward in advising one to go to war or to engage in any conflict.

110 يَدَلَّك عَلَى الكُون مِن لا يَكَاوَن

He shows you the way to fight who will not fight (with you, *i.e.*, on your side).

كَاوَن 'Om.=he fought. كُون 'Om.=a fight.

Same in application as the last proverb.

اَلدَّوْم الْعَبَل يَقَصّ الْحَجِر   111

(If) always, (even) a rope cuts through a stone.

Eng. eq. Constant dropping wears the stone.

يَذْكُرو الْبُلْدَان جَأْت قَيْقَا مُدَوْلَة   112

They are talking of towns and cities, and (suddenly) mention is
made of the troops of Kaiká. Kaiká is an unimportant place in
' Omán.

Applied when a person makes mention suddenly of an unimportant
matter while people are talking over serious affairs.

ذَمّة رَأس الْمَال   113

Credit is capital. ذَمّة ' Om. = credit.

To a merchant credit is as good as capital.

رَابِع الْكَذَّاب إِلَى رِزّ الْبَاب   114

Accompany a liar to the threshold of the door.

If one takes the trouble of following or examining a liar, the false-
hood of his statement will soon become apparent.

Eng. eq. Pretenders should be put to the test. Conf. B. A. P.,
No. 99.

رَاعِى الطَّبَع مَا يَصْبِر عَن طَبْعَه وَلَو يَقَص صَبْعَه   115

A person endowed with a particular kind of nature cannot hide it
even if his finger is cut off. (*Lit.* he is impatient to show it.)

Nature will assert itself.

رَجْل بِلَا حِيلَة كَمَا تَفَق بِلَا فَتِيلَة   116

A man without machination (cunning) is like a matchlock without a
match.

تَفَق ' Om. = a matchlock, a gun.

الرَّدَّة أَكْثَرُ عَنِ الضَّغْوَة   117

A purse-net (raddeh) may catch more (fish) than a seine (dagweh). A raddeh is a small supplementary net attached to the dagweh to catch such fish as may escape the latter.

A small dependent person may sometimes accomplish more than a big and independent one.

رِزْق الكِلَاب عَلَى المَجَانِين   118

Dogs are dependent for their food on madmen.

Applied to persons who waste the good things of this world. Conf. B. A. P., No. 293.

رَكَب الهَزِيلَة لِتَلْحَق السَّمِينَة   119

Ride the lean one (she-camel) that you may overtake the fat one.

It is better even to ride an emaciated camel for the purpose of over-taking a good one that has been lost than to go on foot without any chance of meeting it.

On the advisability of taking advantage of an opportunity even if it be a weak one.

الرُّنْز غَرْقِي والكَيِّيل عَوَر   120

The rice is damaged (lit. such as has been in water) and the measurer blind.

A double calamity; also employed in the sense of two bad things matching each other. Conf. B. A. P., No. 618.

رُوحَك تَدَوِّر عِجَوِلَات الأَصْف   121

You yourself hunt after (lit. try to find) calves by halves.

Applied to a person who brings a misfortune on himself by his own act.

It is usual in 'Omán for the owner of a calf or a kid to make it over to another person for rearing it, and when the calf or kid has grown, the person rearing it shares half the proceeds of its sale with the real owner.

تَزْكِيَةُ النَّفْسِ قَبِيحَة ١٢٢

Self-praise is disdainful (ugly).

Eng. eq. Self-exaltation is the fool's paradise.

زَمَانٍ تَشْكِي مِنَّهُ تَثْنِي تَبْكِي عَلَيْه ١٢٣

When the times you complain of (*lit.* turn aside) pass away, you will cry (wish) for them.

Better to be contented than to grumble about the times we are living in for fear of falling upon worse ones.

زِيد البِلا بِالبِلا اِمّا زَادَ وَاِمّا انْجَلَى ١٢٤

Add trouble to trouble, it will either grow or go.

Eng. eq. Without danger, danger cannot be surmounted.

سَارَت تَبْغِي قُرُون جَأَت بِلا ذُنَين ١٢٥

She (she-goat) went to get horns and returned without ears.

' Om. for ذُنَين = two ears.

Applied to a discontented person who in attempting to overcome a supposed misfortune meets with a more serious one, or in trying to get more loses what he has.

Eng. eq. Many go out for wool and come home shorn.

سَارَت تَبْكِي صَوْت جَأَتْهَا عَبْرَة ١٢٦

She went only to sing (*lit.* cry) a tune but (actually) shed tears.

Trifles lead to serious matters.

A joke or what may be only affected may sometimes end seriously or in reality. In 'Omán women paying visits of condolence are supposed to join the female mourners in crying to an air or tune in praise of the deceased person without actually feeling for his death.

سَارَت تَبُول نَشِيت تَحْت الطَّبُول ١٢٧

She went to micturate, but turned up where the drums were beating.

Applied to trivial pretexts made for attaining important objects.

ساٰيرة تَبْنِى الدَّرٰا جٰاهٰا البَرْد مِن وَرٰا   128

She went to build protection or shelter (from before), but the cold came in from behind.

Applied to a person whom misfortunes befall notwithstanding his efforts to surmount them. It is also applied to one who does exactly opposite of what he ought to do.

ساٰيرة تِرُبِى نُحِّت فِي الغَبِّي   129

She went to be confined, but turned up in al-Gabbee. Al-Gabbee is the name of a place in the Dáhireh at a distance from 'Omán Proper.

Applied to a person who employs a pretext of some kind for going away. It may also be used in the sense of proverb No. 127.

سجِّلهٰا ولٰا تَقسِّلهٰا   130

You had better prop it up (a female date-palm) than plant a new one (in its place).

This is generally given as advice to one who is impatient with his wife. It is better to put up with her weaknesses than to commence life anew by taking a new one.

Eng. eq. Better to bear with the adversities you have than to fly to others ye wot not of.

سِجِلَّة ' Om. = a prop generally made of the trunk of a date-palm and a cross-stick to support a falling palm.

سِكِن عَلَى المٰا ولٰا تَسأٰل عَن رِزق   131

Live near water and ask not about sustenance.

Wherever there is fresh water there is sure to be enough of food.

سَلُم رٰاعِي المَصرِيَة وطٰاحَت فِي رٰاعِي القَضٰاعِية   132

The man with the donkey escaped, and she (the female spirit) seized the man of Kadá'iyeh. Origin of the proverb.—A man went out one night riding a donkey and met a female spirit, who also mounted the donkey behind him. The man was frightened and could not even stir in his seat. The spirit then dismounting led the donkey about here and there during the night until they arrived near Kadá'iyeh, where a man was engaged in drawing water. The spirit screamed out loudly at the place, upon which the man at the well shouted out عَظْم حَلْقِشْ (May a bone stick in your throat !). She thereupon left the man on the donkey, and proceeding to the man at the well slapped him in the face, the latter immediately falling down and dying on the spot.

Applied to one who escapes a misfortune or calamity at the expense of another person.

Kadá'iyeh is the name of a place near Bidbid in the Simáil Valley.

السَّمَا مَا تَغَطَّا بِمُوخَل   133

The sky cannot be hidden with a sieve. مُوخَل 'Om. for مُنْخَل = a sieve.

Applied in the sense of inappropriateness of things and also of an impossibility.

Eng. eqs. Murder will out. He draws water with a sieve.

السَّمَّة رُقْعَتْهَا الخَصَفْ   134

The (proper) patch for mending a date-palm mat is a piece of a date-palm bag.

Lowly pursuits become lowly men.

سَمَّة وعَجَان قَالُوا ضَعَنْ — بِيت لِجَعَارِيف قَالُوا حِصَنْ   135

A date-palm leaf mat and a staff with a hooked head :—they said, "household furniture." A nest of black ants :—they said, "a fort."

To a goat-herd his staff with the bent head for drawing down branches of trees and a palm leaf mat for collecting leaves upon, are his household furniture, whilst to the black ants their ant-hill of earth is a fort.

Every one has things in proportion to his position and capacity.

عَجَان stands for عَجِين . جَعَارِيف *pl.* of جَعْرُوف 'Om.=the black ant (*Componotus compressus*).

سِيرِ بَعِيد رِتَعَالْ سَالِم   136

Go by a distant way, but come safe.

Eng. eq. Better go about than fall into the ditch.

$$ \text{السيف قبضه ضاربه} \quad 137 $$

Hand over the sword to its striker.

Applied in the sense of entrusting an affair to a proper or capable person.

Eng. eq. Every man to his trade.

$$ \text{سيما خت مكزح} \quad 138 $$

Seimá is the sister of Mukazzah. خت for أُخْت

Applied to two things or persons much about the same in appearance or quality.

Seimá and *Mukazzah* are two small villages in the valley of Beni-Ruwáheh in ' Omán Proper, and are close to and like each other.

$$ \text{شاة من قادها وغويز من ردة} \quad 139 $$

A she-goat whom anybody can lead, or a small water channel which anybody can turn.

غويز *dim.* of غيز ' Om. = a water channel.

Applied to a person who can be easily led astray, or one who is not of a firm mind.

$$ \text{شاردة ولا قبة مهباط} \quad 140 $$

She (a she-camel) wanted to run away and (in the meantime) came on a slope.

Applied to a person who meets with circumstances favourable to his design.

$$ \text{الشاكي جنيبي والقاضي مخروقي} \quad 141 $$

The complainant is a Jineibee and the judge a Mahrookee.

Where the complainant and the judge belong to the same tribe, the result may be expected to be in favour of the complainant. *Al-Maháreek* is a *fakheedeh* or sub-tribe of the *Jineibeh*.

142 شايفين مسكد و فرضها ما نستعجب من مصرية تسحب غرضها

We have seen Maskat and its custom houses, and are not (therefore) astonished at the sight of a female donkey dragging her girth.

Employed when a person has seen more wonderful things than those he is shown as objects of admiration. Conf. Nos. 24 and 25.

143 شجرة ما تظل عرفها اولى قصها

It is better to cut off a tree which does not shade its own rootlets.

On the advisability of giving up the friendship of a person who does not give any protection or help.

144 شراطة عند الحياسة ولا نزاعة عند الدروسة

Conditions ought to be made at the time of ploughing, so that there may be no quarreling at the time of treading out (grain).

It is better to have a distinct understanding between all parties at the commencement of a business than to quarrel needlessly in the middle of it or afterwards.

145 الشرط غالب السالفة — الشرط يغلب السالفة

A condition outweighs a rule or custom.

If two persons have agreed upon a condition contrary to a rule or custom of a place, the arbitrators must decide between them according to the condition.

سالفة 'Om. = a rule, a truce.

146 اشتري فضة رغاف ذهب

Buy silver and cover (it) with gold. Conf. No. 45.

147 شل الزاد الى توصل البلاد

Take sufficient provisions (to last you) till you reach the town or country.

On the advisability of making the necessary preparations before commencing a business.

148   شَلّ فِى الدّيِك قَبِل مِن تَجِى أَذِى وَأَذِيك

Be warned by (the loss of) a cock before this or that (misfortune)
attacks (you).

أَذِي and أَذِيك stand for هَـٰذِي and هَـٰذِيك 'Om. *fem.* forms
for *this* and *that.*

Be warned by a small misfortune before greater ones befall you.

149   شَمِج وِلَا بِن عَم

Better (to have) a brother-in-law (or a wife's relation) than a cousin
(or a blood relation).

A person is likely to get more assistance from the former, because
he would be interested in the welfare of his sister.

150   شِي شِي نَاقَة حَمَّت عَلَى وَلَد غَيرِها

No she-camel yearns for the young one of another.

Every one for himself.

شِي شِي 'Om. = no, not any.

151   شِيلَا بِيلَا لَا بِيَاذَيلَا وِلَا بِيَاذَيلَا

Mixed up, neither with these nor with those.

Used to express an affair or a thing mixed up, neither good nor
bad ; also applied to persons.

شِيلَا بِيلَا is a common mercantile expression in seaport towns,
applied chiefly to grain, such as rice, wheat, &c., meaning that the
commodity is mixed up, the purchaser not having the option of selecting the good part and rejecting the bad one. It is evidently derived
from Gujarati એળ સેળ = *commixture* or છેલ = last and ભેળ = mixed.
بِيا is the 'Om. form of بِ = with. ذَيلَا stands for هَـٰذَيلَا 'Om. = these.

152   صَبُر عَن مَجنُونَك اَن يَجِيك اَجَن عَنّه

Be patient with your madman lest you may have one madder still.

Bear your misfortunes patiently, for in attempting to overcome them
you may meet with worse ones.

153   صَدِيق أَبُوكَ لَا تَجَافِي or لَا تَعَادِي

Do not offend or injure your father's friend.

A young man whose father is dead is generally advised to be guided by the advice of his father's friend and not to offend him in any way.

154   صَدِيق مُخَسِّر عَدُو مُبْلِس

A friend that causes a loss is decidedly an enemy.

A foolish friend may prove to be worse than an open enemy.

155   صَغَارِهُم فُلْفُل وَكِبَارِهُم زَنْجِبِيل

Their little ones are pepper and their elders ginger.

Applied to people noted for their courage and power.

156   ضَارُب فِي العِزِّ وَ ذَلَّ مَذْرُوكَ

Fight for honour, for disgrace can be obtained (at any time).

A person is advised to fight or exert himself for some object which will bring him glory, whilst disgrace can be gained without any exertion.

Eng. eq. (of the latter part). From fame to infamy is a beaten road.

157   ضَرَبْنِي وَبَكَى سَبَقْنِي وَشَكَى

He beat me and cried out and preceded me and complained (against me).

Applied to one who is himself the cause of a complaint, but is foremost in accusing others.

Eng. eq. The offender never pardons. Conf. B. A. P., No. 385.

158   الضَّرْب فِي غَيْرَكَ كَشَقّ فِي الجِدَار

The beating which another person receives is (to you) like a cleft in a wall.

What pains others does not pain you.

Eng. eq. None can feel the weight of another's burden.

ضْرُب كَلْبَك بِيَعْرِف جَارَك   159

Beat your dog, so that your neighbour may know (your wish).

If one is pestered by visits from a person whom he does not want,
an indirect expression of anger used to a servant or other attendants,
would be a sure means of getting rid of the unwelcome visitor.   Conf.
F. A. P., Caput I, No. 187.

مَضْرُوب فِي الرَّاس طَشّ المُخّ مِن الرُّكَبَة   160

He was beaten in the head, but the brain came (*lit.* jumped) out of
the knee.

Applied to a sudden or an unexpected event.   Thus when a person
suddenly or unexpectedly startles with an unimportant proposition or
piece of news, a company who are deliberating over a serious affair.

مُخّ ' Om. = brain.   رُكَعَة ' Om. = a knee.   طَشّ ' Om. = he jumped.

ضُمّ مَالَك ولا تَتَّهِم جَارَك   161

Take care of (*lit.* conceal) your property, and accuse not your
neighbour.

Place your property in a safe position, so that there may be no occasion for accusing anybody of having stolen it.

Eng. eq. Safe bind, safe find.

طَالِبَة انواحِم كَلَتْ المَربِيَّة   162

The pregnant one (woman) asked for it, but the confined one ate it.

On the misapplication of things.   وَاحِم ' Om. = pregnant.   المَربِيَّة
from رَبَتْ ' Om. = she was confined.

طَالِع مِن الخَبّ طَاح فِي الطَّوِي   163

He came out of the *khabb*, but fell into the well.

الخَبّ ' Om. = the inclined plane before a well over which a bullock
goes up and down in drawing water.

طَالِعْ مِن القَوْم مِرْتُوه الغَزَّايَة 164

He escaped from the main body of the troops, but was plundered by a party of raiders.

القَوْم ' Om. = a large body of troops. It is usual for them on a march to plunder everybody they come across, unless he belongs to one of the tribes to which they belong or is protected by a man of one of the friendly tribes.

طَالِعْ مِن المَوْت طَاح فِي حَضْرَمَوْت 165

He escaped from death, but fell into Hadramaut.

All these three proverbs (Nos. 163, 164, and 165) are similar to one another in application.

Eng. eq. From the frying pan into the fire.

مَطْرُد مِن البِلَاد كَيْف يَسْكِن فِي الفَوَاد 166

Driven away from the town or country, how can he be quiet in his heart.

A banished person is not likely to remain quiet in his banishment.

الطَّيْر يَحُطّ عَلَى الحَبّ مَا يَحُطّ عَلَى القَبّ 167

Birds alight on grain and not on a staff.

Take by persuasion, not by force.

الظَّالِم مَا يَفْلَح 168

A tyrant does not prosper.

Similar in application to No. 74.

ظِرْصُه خَصِينُه وِ بَطْنُه سَحْصِينُه 169

His tooth is his axe and his stomach his store basket.

فِرْس stands for ظِرْص and مِحَصّ for سَحْصِينِى

Applied to one who possesses nothing.

عُدّ مَوْج البَحْرِ الجَايَاتِ اَكْثُر عَنِ السَّايِرَاتِ　　170

Count the waves of the sea, the comers are more than the goers.

Employed in the case of a person who has committed a fault and on behalf of whom pardon has been asked but refused ; this proverb is then used as a last argument to obtain pardon for that occasion, as chances for punishment are sure to present themselves again. It is also used as a consolation to a person who has lost any valuable thing. Conf. F. A P. Tom III, No. 1937.

العَطْشَانَة تَكْسِرِ الحَوْض　　171

A thirsty one (she-camel) breaks the tank of water (to get at it).

Applied in the sense of want of patience on the part of a needy person.

Eng. eq. A hungry man, an angry man.

عَطِى المَرِيض شَهْوَتُة وقُولُ عَافَاكَ اللَّه　　172

Give the sick man what he desires and say, " May God give you health!"

Used by a person when he is in great need of a thing and asks it as a favour.

عَقّ حَصَاةٍ إلَى طِيَاحَهَا فَلَكَ　　173

Throw a stone ; (perchance) by the time it falls (to the ground) the wheel of fortune will have revolved.

Employed in consoling persons who are found in deep and anxious thoughts. Origin of the proverb.—It is related that Nu'mán bin Mundhir used to consider a certain number of days unlucky and the others lucky, and that it was his habit during the unlucky period if anybody spoke to him to order his head to be cut off. Now, Nu'mán had an intimate friend living at some distance from him ; he died leaving a son, who in order to ingratiate himself into the favour of the king used to send him costly presents. This young man having been advised by his mother to visit the king personally repaired to him, but was not aware of his custom of beheading everybody that spoke to him on his unlucky days. It happened that the day on which the young man visited the king was one of his unlucky days, and the latter therefore ordered his head to be struck off when he saluted him. After a great deal of entreaty the young man obtained a respite of a certain number of days to enable him to arrange his affairs before dying, on condition of his giving a security who should undergo the penalty in the event of his not returning within the time. An old man stood as his security, and the young man went away to arrange his affairs. On the last day of the respite the young man not having returned, the old man was ordered to undergo the punishment, but he asked as a favour that it may be put off till sunset and said, " Throw a stone ; (perchance) by the time it falls (to the ground), the wheel of fortune will have revolved." A stone was therefore thrown up, and by the time it could come down to the ground, the young man returned and also the sun set, and as that was the last day of the unlucky period, both the men escaped with their lives. Conf. Ál-Meydánee's version of the narrative, F. A. P., Caput I, No. 361, and Sale's Translation of the Kurán, Preliminary Discourse.

تَعَلَّم الكَسَانَة عَلَى رُوُس المَجَانِين 174

Learn to shave on the heads of madmen.

Applied in the sense of experimenting first on valueless or worthless things.

حَسَن ' Om. = he shaved.

عَلَيك بالبَزَّل ولَو هَزَّل 175

You have (only) to look to the purity or good origin (of a thing) even if it be thin or emaciated.

On the principal point to be borne in mind in selecting a wife or an animal.

عَلَيه سِتّ وكَبشه بِسِتّ 176

There are six (dollars) against him and his sheep is worth six (dollars).

Eng. eq. Six of one and half-a-dozen of the other.

عِند الحَصَايد يَدُور القَصَايد 177

At the time of harvest he goes about singing songs.

Applied to one who wastes his time in vain and frivolous things when there is an important business on hand.

178   عِنْد الخُطْبَة اللسَان رُطْبَة وخلاف تِيبَس كَمَا الحَطَبَة

At the time of asking in marriage the tongue is moist, but afterwards it dries up like wood.

While one is in need of a thing sweet promises are made, but
directly the object is gained they are all forgotten.

Eng. eq. Vows made in storms are forgotten in calms.

179   عِنْدِى اللَّحْم مَا اصِيد الرِّخِيم

I have meat ; I shall not hunt vultures. Said by a person who has
good things in his possession and need not therefore trouble himself
about getting any inferior ones.

180   عُورَا تَقُود رَمْدَانَة

A blind woman leading one suffering from ophthalmia.

The blind leading the blind.

181   العَيْرِيَّة تَزْهَا ولَا تَدُوم

A borrowed thing may appear beautiful, but (the possession of it)
does not last.

Ever so beautiful a borrowed thing may be, it must sooner or later
pass away from the possession of the borrower of it.

العَيْرِيَّة stands for العَارِيَّة = a loan.

182   العَيْش فِي مَزْوِدِتْنَا والنَّار فِي مَضْرِبْتْنَا والمَاء فِي قَرْبِتْنَا ونَجِى
عِنْد النَّاس عَلَى هَوَانَا وطَرْبِتْنَا

We have food in our food-bag, fire in our pouch, and water in our
water-skin, and we come to people just as we like and please.

Applied to persons who can afford to be independent of others.

183   عَيْنِى غَرِيَّة مِن مَرَق البَرِيَّة

My eye is satiated with (the sight of) the gravy of anchovies.

Applied to one who is sick of a thing from an excess of it.

بَرِيَّة ' Om. = anchovy. *Engraulis commersonianus.*

عَيْنٍ مَا شَافَتَكَ مَا لَا مَتَكَ ١٨٤

The eye that does not see you does not blame you.

Eng. eq. What the eye sees not the heart rues not.

غَابَت السّكْرَة وِجَأَت الفَكْرَة ١٨٥

The intoxication has passed away and anxiety has come.

Applied to pain after pleasure and penury after plentifulness. Conf.
B. A. P., No. 292.

الغَالِي مَا يَبْتَاع مَرّتَيْن ١٨٦

What is dear (in price) cannot be sold twice (at the same high price).

This proverb is generally used in reply to a shopkeeper who says that
he himself has purchased a certain thing dear.

غَضًّا بِيَدَيْك وِلَا نَضِيجاً بِيد غَيْرِك ١٨٧

Better a raw thing with your own hands than a ripe one with the
hands of another.

On the advisability of accomplishing a thing oneself, however
clumsily it may be done, instead of depending upon others to do it in a
clever manner.

الغُلَب طُوع ١٨٨

He who is defeated obeys. Conf. F. A. P., Caput XXV, No. 166.

الفُعْل فُعْل النَّذَال وِيَطِيح القَضَى في الرَّجّال ١٨٩

The act is that of the mean, but its consequences fall upon the great
man.

The sheikh of a tribe or the elder of a family is held responsible for
the acts of persons belonging to the tribe or family, however low or
mean they may be in position.

فُنْدَال دَيْوَل قِيسِيه وِشْبْرِيه ١٩٠

A Deiwal sweet potato, compare it (with others) and measure it
with the span. A woman is supposed to be about to buy a sweet
potato and does not know which one to select.

Applied to a person who is confused and unable to decide what
course to adopt.

Deiwal is the name by which the town of Tatta in Sind is known to the ' Omânees, who apply the name Deiwalee Banyans to the Hindus of that province. It is possible that sweet potatoes were imported from Sind in old days, and that they were very irregular in shape and difficult of being measured or compared with one another.

فُنْدَال ' Om. = sweet potato.

191　في طِرِيقٍ رَابِعٍ مِنْ اَذْرُب عَنَّك

On the road take for a companion (*lit.* accompany) one who is stronger than yourself.

On the advisability of having a strong protector on a journey or in any important undertaking.

رَابِع ' Om. = he accompanied.

192　قَارُوت العَالِي إِذَا طَلَع الفُلَع قَالَت حَالِي

(Like) Károot al-'álee which whenever a new spring is discovered (*lit.* comes out) says, " It is mine."

Applied to a person who grabs everything he can get hold of, even on the ground of a fictitious claim.

Upper *Károot* is a village in the valley of the Beni-Ruwáheh, the people of which lay a claim to every spring that is found in its vicinity on the ground of its being a feeder of their own springs which, they allege, would dry if the new one is utilized in any other direction.

193　قَبٌّ وحِزَاق والرَّبُّ رِزَّاق

A club and a waist-wrapper, and the Lord is the provider.

Applied to an improvident person who does not care or trouble himself about earning his livelihood.

حِزَاق ' Om. = a waist-wrapper.

194　قَدِيم البُرَيْسُم ولا جَدِيد الصُّوف

Better old silk than new wool.

It is better to have a valuable friend or thing though old than a valueless friend or thing though new.

قُرِّيْن وَازِع مُغَتِّل عَلَى سِمَايِل 195

Karein Wázu'a overshades *Simáil.*

Applied to a defect or a drawback in a person or thing.

Eng. eq. One scabbed sheep mars a flock.

Karein Wázu'a was a lofty fortified building on a hill in the town of Simáil, and used to overshade all the date-palm plantations underneath it, thus preventing the trees from having a vigorous growth. It was pulled down in 1876 by an order of the late Sultan of Maskat.

مُغَتِّل from غَتَل ' Om. = it shaded or overshaded.

196 كَان تَبْغَى تَصَلَّى مَا تُغْلَب or مَا تَعَايَل

If you want to pray, you cannot be prevented (*lit.* overcome).

Eng. eq. Where there is a will there is always a way.

197 كَان يَبْغَى يَمُوت وِسْمُه

If he wants to die, brand him. كَان stands for إِن كَان = if.

Said of one who is already suffering from an affliction, and to whom any additional pain would be a sure cause of his ruin or death. Branding is a common remedy in 'Oman and is resorted to even for trivial complaints.

198 كَان بَغَيْت الوَلَد نَقِّي لُه جِدًّا وخَال

If you want a good son, select for him a good (maternal) grandfather and a good (maternal) uncle. نَقَّى 'Om. = he selected.

On the selection of a good wife.

199 كَان تَجِي عَقَبَة وكَان تَجِي ظَيْت مِلْتَقَا فِي رِيَام

Whether you come by the pass or over the rocks the meeting place would be Riyám. عَقَبَة 'Om. = a pass. ظَيْت = a rock. Both the roads mentioned in the proverb on the way from Matrah to Maskat meet at Riyám.

Said when the result is likely to be the same whichever way a thing is done.

200   كان مستنضر من جبر و كيف يشيع له في ريام

If he has been attacked by an evil spirit at Jabroo, how can the
remedial measures be adopted in Riyám? *Jabroo* is a suburb of
Matrah, and *Riyám* a village on the way from Matrah to Maskat.

مضرّة ' Om. = condition of a person attacked by an evil spirit. يشيع له

' Om. = an offering of food and incense was made to an evil spirit.

On the unsuitableness of two things to each other.

201   كان ما شي طحين عصده

If there be no flour, prepare '*aseedeh* of it. '*Aseedeh* is a sort of
thick gruel the principal constituent of which is wheat flour.

Applied to a person who asks for a greater thing than the one for
which his request has been already refused. It is generally applied
to an impudent beggar.

Refused a crust, he demanded a loaf.

202   كبره كبر نخلة وعقله عقل سخلة

His size is that of a date-palm, but his reasoning (intelligence) that
of a kid.

Applied to one who has a large body but a small brain, —a fool.
Conf. F. A. P., Tom. III, No. 1856.

203   الكثرة تغلب الشجعان

Numbers overpower the brave.

204   كثير في العزاف غم في البطن

Plenty on the table, but sadness in the stomach.

Applied to a thing which is plentiful but profitless. Quantity without quality. *Sadness in the stomach* on account of the food being
plentiful but not of the quality to benefit the person eating it.

عزاف ' Om. = a small round mat on which the tray containing the
several articles of food is placed. It is called also in some parts
سفرة and in others كفار.

205 كُدِّي يَا غُزَالَة وِلِّي يَا سِبَالَة

Toil away, O Gazelle, and eat away, O Monkey.

Used when a good person of rank works hard, and a wretched worthless fellow enjoys the fruit of the work; for instance, the master or lady of a house may work hard to earn money, whilst a slave or a lazy worthless member of the family derives the benefit of it.

سِبَال ' Om. = a monkey.

Eng. eq. Masters are generally the greatest servants in the house.

206 كَالسَّيفِ فِي قَطَاعَتَه والرَّجِل بِيَا رِبَاعَتَه

Like a sword in its scabbard or a man with his friends.

Applied to an untried person or thing.

Eng. eq. Judge not a ship as she lies on the stocks.

207 كَعُوِرْ بِيَاق يِكِّر رِشبَنَّه ويلُوح عِسقَتَه

Like the blind man of Biyák who is always replenishing his *hookah* with water and waving the date-stalk about (to kindle a fire). رِشبَنَّه

' Om. = a *hookah. Biyak* = a village in the valley of Beni-Ruwáheh.

Eng. eq. Many sift night and day, and yet get nothing but bran.

208 كَفْ وَاحِدَة مَا يُصَفِق

One palm of the hand does not cause a clapping of hands.

Eng. eq. 'Tis the second blow that makes a fray.

209 كَلَام الوَطَا أَحسَن مِن العَطَا

Humble words are better than a gift. وَطَا *pl.* of وَطِي ' Om. = low.

210 كَلب بَيْن كَلبَيْن ذَلِيل بَيْن ثَلَاث قَتِيل

A dog between two dogs is a coward and among three dogs is killed.

The greater the number is of rivals in a field, the less the chance is of a man being bold or successful.

كَلْب دَايِر ولَا أَسَد رَاقِد   211

Better a roving dog than a sleeping lion.

Eng. eq. A living dog is better than a dead lion.

كُلّ تَعْسِيرَة فِيهَا خِيرَة   212

In every difficulty there is a blessing.

Used in the sense of consolation when one meets with a difficulty or disappointment.

كُلّ حَد كِسَاحَتَه قُدَّام بَيْتَه   213

Everyone has his sweepings in front of his house.

Every one has his faults and defects before him. كُلّ حَد stands for كُلّ أَحَد and كِسَاحَة for كِسَاحَتَه.

Eng. eq. Every light has its shadow.

كُلّ حَلّة فِيهَا عِلّة   214

Every quarter (of a town or village) has some drawback or another.

Eng. eq. Every bean hath its black.

كُلّ مَحْصُور مَاخُوذ   215

Everything or everyone that is besieged is taken or conquered.

A besieging enemy has only to wait patiently for a besieged place to fall.

كُلّ ذَنْبَه عَلَى جَنْبَه   216

Everyone has (the responsibility of) his crime upon himself.

Everyone must himself suffer the penalty of his fault.

Eng. eq. Every herring must hang by its own head.

كُلّ سَاقِطَة اِلَهَا رَاقِطَة وكُلّ عَاجِزَة اِلَهَا بَخْت   217

For everything that drops there is a picker-up and for every spinster there is luck.

رَاقِطَة stands for لَاقِطَة, اِلَهَا for لَهَا, and عَاجِزَة perhaps for عَازِبَة.

Eng. eq. No pot is so ugly as not to find a cover.

كُلّ شَارُب إِلهُ مُقَصّ   218

Every moustache has its scissors.

Applied to the adaptation of things.

كُلّ بِعَقْلَه رَاضِي وعَمّا مَالَه لَا   219

Everyone is pleased with his reasoning (intelligence) but not so in regard to his wealth.

Everyone is contented with his intellectual powers but not with the wealth he possesses.

كُلّ كَمَا كُلّ جَا الهَبُوب وشَلّه   220

All (the dust) is alike ; the wind came and took it away. هَبُوب
'Om. = wind.

Applied to persons or things all equally bad.

كُلْمَة الَّتِي نَتْخَجّل مِنْهَا بَدّ يهَا قَبل   221

Mention first the word you are ashamed or shy about.

All disagreeable conditions ought to be settled before commencing a business.

Eng. eq. A word before is worth two behind.

كُلّ يِمْدَح سُوقًا رِبِح فِيه   222

Everyone praises a market in which there is a profit (for himself).

كَمَا بُو يِدُور جَمَل خَالَته مِن لَقِيه رِكِب وغَنّى ومِن مَا لَقِيه   223
مِشَى وغَنّى

Like one who searches for his aunt's camel ; if he finds it, he rides and sings ; and if he does not find it, he walks and sings. مِن
stands for اِذَا.

Applied to a person who is sent in search of a thing or to do a business in which he takes no interest.

224   كَمَا سَنُّورُ أَدَم مِن شَلَّيْتَه مَن وَمِن وَدَّرْتَه مَن

Like the cat of Adam which if you lifted up was a maund in weight
and which if you left alone was (still) a maund in weight.

This proverb can be used in two senses. First, in the sense of the
Eng. eq. A rolling stone gathers no moss. Secondly, in the sense of
an ungrateful or a naturally bad person who is not affected by the
kind of treatment he receives at the hands of people.

Adam is the name of a town in 'Omán Proper, where a lean and
miserable cat once lived; it used to go about in the town, and whether
it was fed well or not it never changed in its weight.

225   كَمَا ضَاضُوَة العُوْرَا يَجِيها الرِّزْق إِلَى مِنْقَابها

Like the blind Roller to whose beak food finds its way.

Applied to a person who cannot exert himself and has to depend
upon others for food.

ضَاضُوَة 'Om.= Indian roller—*Coracias indica.*

226   كَمَا قَصَّاب نَزْوَى

Like a butcher of Nazwá.

Applied to a discontented person who always complains of a loss in
his business or other matter.

The butchers of Nazwá are noted for complaining of a loss, though
there may be an undoubted proof of the case being the opposite of it.

One of them was once given a bullock for nothing and told to
slaughter it and sell the meat for his own benefit. On being question-
ed as to the result, he complained of having suffered a loss though he
had not to pay anything as the price of the bullock, and explained that
the wear of his knives had also to be taken into consideration. Nazwá
is a large important town in 'Omán and was at one time its capital.

227   لَا تَأَمَّن مِنِ الثُّور وَلَو رَاسُه فِي التَّنُّور

Do not trust a bull even if its head be in an oven.

A caution against trusting a dangerous enemy even if he has fallen.

لَا حَامِض يَجْلِي الكِبْد وَلَا الاَحْمَر يَفَرِّحُوبَه الصَّغِيرِين ‏ 228

Neither an acid thing to clear the liver, nor a red thing to gladden children.

Said of a useless thing or person.

لَبَّيْكَ يَا نَافِع وِلَوُ سَاحِر ‏ 229

Here I am, O (my) benefactor, even if you are an enchanter (oppressor). In 'Omán enchanters are looked upon as oppressors of mankind.

The call of one's benefactor is readily answered even if he be a wicked man.

اللَّحم حَالُ السَّحَر وَالدَّعوا على المطيطورة ‏ 230

The meat is for the sorcerers or enchanters, whilst the curse falls on the (poor) lapwing. مطيطورة 'Om. = a lapwing—*Lobivanellus goensis.*

The people of 'Omán generally have a firm belief in sorcery or enchantment, which is supposed to be in many instances the cause of disease and death. Enchanters are supposed to have three animals in their service, namely, ضبِع *fem.* ضبعون (hyena), مقعاشة (fox), and مطيطو (lapwing), which last acts as their messenger. The cry of this bird is looked upon as a very inauspicious omen, and the hearer of it always curses the bird with the phrase عظم حَلقِش (May a bone stick in thy throat!). The cries of certain other animals are also looked upon as omens. Thus the cry of a cow is considered an inauspicious one, and is replied to by the curse على قرونش (On thy horns may the danger fall!); the cry of a donkey is auspicious, and is replied to by the benediction خِيرِ يَا بو خُضَير (Mayest thou prosper, O harbinger of plenty!); the cry of a camel is judged according to its nature; if affectionate and tender it is considered auspicious, and if it be like a groan inauspicious, the phrase used in either case in reply being حَنِينَش وِلَا نِينَش. (Let us have thy affectionate cry but none of thy groaning).

In the proverb the poor bird is cursed as being the messenger of the enchanters, who are supposed to be at a distance enjoying themselves on meat and unaffected by the curse.

The carrier of a disagreeable message is exposed to ill-treatment whilst the sender of it is safe at a distance.

231 لِيَدْخُل بَيْن البَصَل والثُّوم يَطْلَع خَايِس ومَدْمُوم

He who enters among onions and garlic comes out stinking and in a contemptible plight.

Eng. eq. He that lies with dogs must expect to rise with fleas.

232 لَقْمَة ولَا بُرْمَة

Better a morsel (ready cooked) than an (empty) earthen cooking pot.

It is better to have something which is likely to be of immediate use even if it be a little, than to have much of what is useless.

بُرْمَة ' Om. = an earthen cooking vessel.

Eng. eq. A bird in hand is worth two in the bush.

233 لَو سِنْد فِيهَا خَيْر سَدَّت دَرَاوِيشهَا or كَفَّت سِنُودَهَا

If there was any good in Sind, it (Sind) would have been enough for its Darweishes or Sindees.

Applied to a useless person who is not able to help himself for want of good qualities in him, much less those who depend on him.

234 لَو تَرْكُض رَكَض الوُحُوش غَيْر رِزْقَك مَا تَحُوش

Even if you run at the rate that wild animals do, you will not get more than your (predestined share of) means of sustenance.

Applied in the sense of the preponderance of one's luck over his exertions.

235 لَو مَا الدَّهُوج مَا نَفَقَت الخُمَامَة

If there were no fools, rubbish (sweepings) would not be sold (*lit.* spent or used up). Conf. No. 118.

236 لِى يَجْرِي عَلَى التَّعِيبَة يَجْرِي عَلَى المُتَهَنِّيَة

What happens to one in poor or embarrassed circumstances happens also to one in easy circumstances.

لِي مَا يَأْدِبُهُ أَهْلُهُ يَأْدِبُهُ الزَّمَانُ 237

He who is not taught (discipline) by his people, is taught by fortune (time).

Experience of the world and vicissitudes of fortune soon teach one how to behave himself, if he has not already learnt to do it.

مَا بَادَلْ بِمَحْبُوب الحَشَا جِنّى 238

One does not exchange a sweetheart for a *jinnee* (evil spirit).

One does not exchange a good thing or a favourite person for one that is bad and disliked.

مَاتَت الحِمَارَة وَانْقَطَعَت الزَّوَارَة 239

The donkey is dead and the visiting is over.

Applied to an ungrateful person who ceases paying visits when his purpose is gained.

مَا يَحِكّ شَفْرِي اِلَّا ظَفْرِي 240

Nothing or nobody can scratch my lip but my own nail.

Nobody can do one's work so well as himself.

مَا دَام زَاجِيَة بْنِزجِيهَا وِيُوم تَزْجِي شِي حَنِّجِي شِي 241

While it passes (can be palmed off), we shall make it pass ; but when it won't pass (cannot be palmed off), we shall not come.

Origin.—It is related that an uneducated man once went to a village and set up there as a teacher. A short time after, an educated man happening to come there too, the villagers asked him to examine the boys, but he found that they knew nothing, and on his asking the teacher as to how he had taught them, is supposed to have received the above reply.

Applied to one who tries to serve for a time without knowing much about the work he has to do.

شِي 'Om. = not ب and ح are both used in the 'Ománee dialect to indicate the future tense.

242   مَا دَامَ السَّيْل يَسْكُب الحَصَى رُطُب

While the rain pours, the stone is moist.

While fortune smiles, everything that one does is admired. Conf.
No. 35.

243   الماءُ زَائِد عَلَى الطَّحِين

Water more (in proportion) than the flour (in the preparation of
dough).

Applied in the sense of want of proportions.

Eng. eq.   Make not your sail too large for your ship.

244   مَا سَادَّة حَال بَلَّها يَجْبِن مِلْها

It (milk) is not enough for her (the cow's) calf, and he wants to make
cheese out of it.   سَدّ   ' Om. = It was enough.

Applied to one who wants to venture beyond his means.

245   مَا يَسْتَوَى الحَسْب فِي الحَيْل وَالمَحْبُوب رَاكِب خَيْل   or   فِي الغَبْرَة

It cannot be that the sweetheart should be in Hail and the lover on
horseback or at Gobreh.   الحَسْب   stands for   المُحِبّ

On the necessity of certain conditions being present for certain
matters ; thus, according to ' Ománee ideas, it would be difficult for
two lovers to love each other when they are at a distance from each
other.

246   مَا يَسْتَوَى سِيفَيْن فِي قَطَاعَة وَلا سُلْطَانَيْن رَبَاعَة

Two swords cannot be (contained) in one scabbard, nor can two
sultans (reign) together.

Eng. eqs.   Two stars cannot shine in the same hemisphere. One
nail drives out another. Conf. F. A. P., Caput XXIII, No. 365.

247   مَا يَسْتَوَى وَدّرِي بَنْش وِشَلِّى بَنِينَا

" Leave off your child and take up our children," is a thing that
cannot be (done).

Applied to one who proposes an unnatural course, or asks another
person to do his work when that other person has his own work to
attend to.   وَدّر   ' Om. = he abandoned or left.

248   مَا يُشْتَق ثُوْب بَيْن عَاقِلَيْن

Cloth cannot be torn between two wise men.

Friendship between two wise men is not easily broken off.

249   مَا شِي شَرْجَة ضَاقَت بِسَيْلِهَا

There is no watercourse or rivulet which is ever choked by its own flow (water).

No difficulty can be found in adapting two things to each other when they are intended or made for that purpose.

250   مَا شِي صبَّة نَجِت مِن حَشَف

There is no heap (of dates) free from dry and shrivelled ones.

There are black sheep in every flock.

251   مَا يَضَارَب القُوْم غَيْر بُوَيْحَاتِي اللُوْم

Nobody fights an army but he who is afraid of blame.   حَتَّى
' Om. = he was afraid.

Nobody goes willingly to a war. It is the fear of being blamed afterwards as a coward that induces one to do so.

252   مَا طُرْفَة بَاطِنِيَّة فِي غُرْفَة

A Bátineh woman in a room is no wonder.

The women of the Bátineh coast are looked upon as common, and therefore the fact of one of them being in a room (probably as one's wife) is not a matter of wonder.

253   مَا تَطِيح الصَّدِيفَة or السَقِيفَة إلَّا فِي or عَلَى رَأْس الضَعِيفَة

A misfortune or a roof does not fall on the head of any but an unfortunate (weak) person.   صَدِيفَة ' Om. = a calamity.

This proverb is used in the sense of misfortunes generally befalling persons who are already unfortunate or unable to bear them.

Eng. eq. Misfortunes seldom come single.

$$\text{ما نَعْرِفْ مِن حَيّ عَاصُم لَجِرَادِيهَا} \quad 254$$

We do not know Haya ' A'sum from Jarádee.

Applied to two things which cannot be distinguished from each other on account of there being very little difference between them. *Haya ' A'sum* and *Jarádee* are two places on the Bátineh coast so close to each other, that it is difficult to tell the boundary line of one from that of the other. Conf. No. 138.

$$\text{ما يَعْرِف رُطْنِي اّلّا وَلَد بُطْنِي} \quad 255$$

Nobody knows my secret language but my own son.

Eng. eq. The wearer best knows where the shoe pinches.

$$\text{ما يَغِيب دَين غَير بِلّه طَلّاب} \quad 256$$

No debt or claim is lost ; it is sure to have its demanders (sooner or later).

Generally applied to a case of blood revenge,

Origin.—The ' Ománees attribute this proverb to the time of the Prophet ' Eesá (Jesus) who, it is related, one day climbed up a tree on a bank of a river and sat there, when a horseman also happened to come there, and having dismounted from his horse and undressed himself jumped into the river for bathing. After bathing he remounted his horse and went away, forgetting to carry with him a bag of money which he had deposited on the bank of the river. He was shortly after followed by another man, who also selected the same spot for bathing, and on redressing having discovered the bag of money took it away with him. Soon after this a third man came to the same spot, and while he was in the act of bathing, the horseman having by this time discovered his loss returned galloping to the tree and demanded his bag back from the man who was actually bathing at the time. He, however, denied all knowledge of it, and an altercation took place between them, whereupon the horseman drew his sword and slew the other man. " 'Eesá, who had been quietly watching all these events, was greatly astonished and perplexed, upon which a voice from Heaven said, " 'Eesá, do not be astonished ; the forefathers of the horseman were great tyrants and used to force labour from people, while the second man's forefathers were among the labourers who were unpaid, and he had therefore a claim which has now been paid. In the case of the third man one of his forefathers had killed a forefather of the horseman, who has now in retaliation for it killed him. Thus no claim is lost. Sooner or later it is sure to have its demanders."

Conf. story 120th in " نوادر احمد شهاب الدين القليوبي "

257 الْمُغَسِّل مَا يَضْمَن بِالْجَنَّة

The washer of the dead does not guarantee Paradise (to the dead).

Applied in the sense of means to obtain a thing not necessarily meaning success. A person helping one is not bound to bring the thing to a successful issue.

258 مَا كُلّ مَرَّة تَسْلَم الجَرَّة

Not every time is the jar saved.

Eng. eq. A pitcher goes often to the well but is broken at last.

259 مَال الجَبَل حَال الجَمَل ومَال البِجَاب مَاوْرَاة ذِهَاب

The date-palms of a mountainous country belong to the camel, and the date-palms watered with a leathern bucket are in danger of perishing.

Applied to labour without profit, and also to a person between two misfortunes. The first part of the proverb is expressed figuratively, the expense of bringing down the produce of a mountainous country on camel-back being too great to allow of any profit. مَال = property which in 'Omán being composed principally of date-palms, is the name now commonly applied to them. البِجَاب 'Om. = a skin, pl. يُجُب

260 مَال القَرَاح مِن طَاح زَاح

Date-palms planted in sand, when they fall down, are lost. قَرَاح 'Om. = Sandy soil.

Everything founded on unstable ground is in danger of being lost. A weak foundation destroys the superstructure.

261 مَالَك قَدْ تَقْنِي قَال دَ أَيَّة تَشْقَلْنِي

"Why do you beat me?" He said, "Because the cartilages of the breast are splitting me."

Applied to a person who revenges himself upon others than those who have injured him.

مَالَكَ تَصِيمِ قَالَ فِي بَطْنِي رِيح   262

" Why do you bawl out ?" He said, " There is wind in my stomach."
Nobody complains without a reason.

مَالُ مَالَ أَبُوهَا رِيزَوِّدُوهَا فِي سِيعِنَّة   263

The property is her father's, and yet they give her food for the journey
only in a palm-leaf basket.

Applied to one who has no control over his own affairs.

مَا يَنْفَعُكَ غَيْرُ دَمْ عَقْبِيكَ او شَرَا دَرْهَبِيكَ   264

Nothing will benefit you but the blood of your heel (your son), or the
purchase of your money (your slave).

It is only those who are interested in a person's welfare that help
him.

مَا عَلَى الْكَرِيمِ تَشْرُطِ   265

There are no conditions binding on the generous.

Whatever a generous man gives ought to be taken without restrict-
ing him to any conditions.

Eng. eq.   Never look a gift horse in the mouth.

مَا قَاصِرِ عَلَيْنَا لُومِي بِنْعَصِر شَرْجِبَان   266

We are not short of limes that we should squeeze *sharjabán* (Solanum
violaceum).

On substituting a bad thing for a good one which is in abundance.
Limes are abundant in 'Omán, and it would be preposterous to sub-
stitute for them a fruit which only somewhat resembles them in
appearance.

مَالُ الْبُخَّلَا يَاكُلِ الْبُطَّلَا وَمَالِ الْبُطَّلَا حَالِ الشَّيْطَانِ وَالْمُخْزَأ   267

The vain and the useless enjoy the wealth of the stingy, while the
property of the idle and useless belongs to the devil and the vile or
contemptuous.

A miser hoards his wealth to be wasted in immoral and vain pur
poses by his heirs who are generally idle and worthless.

Eng. eq.   The devil lies in the miser's chest.

مِثْقَال مِن الحُكُم وَلَا بَهَار مِن المُرُوَّة 268

A *mithkál* in weight of authority is better than a *bahár* of kindness.

Acts in obedience to orders of persons in authority are more readily performed than those prompted by kindness.

Eng. eq. A friend at court is better than a penny in the purse.

Mithkál = the smallest weight known to the Arabs, equal to a dirham and three-sevenths of a dirham.

Bahár stands for *buhár* = the largest weight known to the 'Ománees, equal to 200 Maskat maunds.

المَلْجُور يَصِيح وَالمَأْشَا لِلَّه رِيح 269

The bucket pulley makes a noise, but the water is carried away by the wind.

Eng. eq. Much ado about nothing.

مَلْجُور ' Om. = a pulley fixed over a well, over which a rope passes for drawing water. Conf. F. A. P., Caput XII. No. 81, and Caput V., No. 13.

مَرِيمُو إِذَا سَدَّت بَابَهَا بَاب اللَّه مَفْتُوح 270

If Mureimo closes her door, the door of God is open.

This proverb is used when a person tries to put off giving help or a gift, by stratagem.

Mureimo was a wily and cunning woman who lived in Wadi Akk in the reign of Sayyid Sultán bin Hamad.

مَسْعُودَة تَأْتِي الخَبَر غَيْر مَنْشُودَة 271

Mas'oodeh brings news without being asked. نَشَد ' Om. = he asked.

Applied to a meddlesome person who interrupts others in conversation.

مَعْنَا القَمَر عَن صِرَاج البَانْيَان 272

We have the moon instead of the Bányán's lamp. صِرَاج ' Om., stands for سِرَاج = a lamp.

A Bányán's lamp is supposed to last much longer and to give brighter light than an Arab's; hence the comparison with it in the proverb, that being the best lamp that an Arab can think of.

273   مِنْ آدَمِي الْحَرْكَة وَمِنْ اللَّه الْبَرْكَة

Action is expected from man and blessing from God.

Eng. eq. Use the means and God will give the blessing.

274   مِنْ الْبَرِّ دُوا حَرْقَاة وَمِنْ الْبَحْرُوا غَرْقَاة

In the direction of land there is fear of being burnt, and in the direction of the sea there is fear of being drowned.

Between two difficulties.

275   مِنْ يَبِيع الْفِجْل يَسْتَاقَى الْعَبَس

He who sells radishes is paid in date-stones.

Eng. eq. As you sow, so you shall reap. مِنْ 'Om. stands for مِنْ=who. عَبَس 'Om. =date-stones. Radishes are generally sold by gardeners, who take payment for them in date-stones on which they feed their cattle. As the selling of radishes is considered a vulgar occupation, so is also the kind of payment for them.

276   مِنْ جَادَ عَادَ

He that gives (anything) out of generosity has it returned.

" He that hath pity upon the poor lendeth unto the Lord ; and that which he hath given will He pay him again." Proverbs, XIX, 17.

277   مِنْ بَغِيْت تَذْكِر فَعَل زِيْن وَلَّا شِيْن

If you wish to be remembered do good or otherwise evil. مِنْ stands for اِنْ=if, and وَلَّا for وَالَّا=otherwise.

278   مِنْ بَغِيْت عَوْنَهَا بَرَّق فِي لَوْنَهَا

If you want the milk a pot full, examine her (the cow's) state (*lit.* colour). Conf. No. 49.

On the advisability of examining a thing or animal carefully before making a purchase.

279 مِن بِنُمِي عَلَى يَدَه قُصَّت

He who has (a wall) built over his hand must have it cut off.

He who meddles with the business of others must suffer for it.

Eng. eq. He that blows in the dust fills his eyes.

280 مِن جِيت مَا بِك فَرَح وِمِن سِرْت مَا مَفْقُود

When you come nobody is glad, and when you go away you are not missed.

Applied to a useless person.

281 مِن حَبِيت طَبِّيت وِمِن بَغَضْت قَلَعْت العِيون

You consider him agreeable whom you love, whilst you pull out the eyes of him whom you hate.

Applied to a person who winks at the faults of those whom he likes and is ready to find fault with those whom he hates.

Eng. eq. (Of the first part.) Love is blind. (Of the latter part.) Faults are thick where love is thin. Conf. F. A. P., Caput XXIV., No. 283.

282 مِن حَشِّت تَعَشِّت

If you cut (grass), you will get your dinner.

On the advisability of working to obtain one's livelihood.

283 مِن يَغَرِّج وِلَا يَحَسِّب يَفْلِس وِلَا يَدْرِى

He who spends and does not calculate, becomes bankrupt and is not aware (of it).

Eng. eq. Who spends before he thrives will starve before he thinks. Conf. F. A. P., Caput XXIV., No. 491.

284 مِن خَصَمَك الجَار اَشْتَل مِن الدَّار

If your neighbour is your enemy, remove from the house.

On avoiding quarrelsome neighbours and keeping aloof from disagreeable things. Conf. B. A. P., No. 9.

285   مِن رَأَيْتَ صَاحِبَكَ يَتَحَسَّن بِل

If you see your friend being shaved apply water (to your own head).

Used in the sense of being warned by the calamities of others.

Similar to مَنْ حُلِقَتْ لَحِيَة جَارِ لَه ــ فَلْيِسْكِب المَاء عَلَى لَحِيتَه = " Let him who has his neighbour's beard shaved pour water over his own beard." Conf. B. A. P., No. 10.

286   مِنَّش رَوَّحَش تَدَوِّرِي الدَّقّ وَلَقَيْتِي

You yourself are the cause (of the misfortune) ; you hunt after beating and have got it.

Said to one who has brought a misfortune on herself and complains of it.

287   مِنَّك رَوَّحَك خَسُوفِيتَك جَرَحَة يَدَك

You yourself are the cause of your injury, the wound of your hand.

Similar to the last one.

288   مِن شَافْ بِعَيْنَه ضَاق ضَيْنَه

He who sees with his eye is straitened in his heart.   ضَيْن ' Om. = heart.

Eng. eq. What the eye sees not the heart rues not.

289   مِن ضَرَب تَبَّه خَذ حَبَّه

He who strikes his staff gets his (share of) wheat.

At harvest time the people that help in beating corn are paid for their trouble in grain.

Eng. eq. No gains without pains.

290   مِن طَمَع طَبَع

He who covets sinks or is drowned.   طَبَع ' Om. = it (a ship) sank.

Eng. eq. The covetous man is his own tormentor. Conf. F. A. P., Tom III., No. 1829.

291 مِن عِنْد الحَبِيب ولو حَبَّة زُبِيب

From a loved one or friend, even if it be a raisin.

A gift from a friend is highly appreciated, even if it be a trifling one.
Conf. B. A. P., No. 387.

292 مِن غَاب عَن العَيْن غَاب عَن القَلْب

He who is not before the eye is absent from the mind.

Eng. eq. Out of sight out of mind.

293 مِن غَلَبش حَبّش كِيلِيه

Owing to the victory (of the times) over you, measure out your grain (to yourself).

Applied to a dull market or want of work owing to hard times. In the proverb the shopkeeper is supposed to be a woman, and is told to amuse herself by measuring out grain to herself for a want of purchasers. ش is the pronominal affix of the second person fem. sing. in the ' Ománee dialect. حَبّ = wheat.

294 مِن كَان لَه حِيلة فلْيحتَال إن الحِيَل مِن شِيَم الرّجَال

Let him who has means of employing a stratagem (to gain his object) do so, for stratagems are (reckoned) among the qualities of good and brave men.

295 مِن لم يفَكّر في العَواقِب مَالَه في الدَّهر صَاحِب

He who does not think of consequences has no friend in the world.

296 مِن نَاخ الجَمَل كثُرَت مَعَالِيقه

When a he-camel lies down its loads increase.

Eng. eq. All lay loads on the willing horse.

297 مِن يتَّكِل عَلَى غَيره يقِل خَيره

He who depends upon another loses his wealth (*lit.* his wealth diminishes).

Eng. eq. Trusting to others' care has been the ruin of many.

298 مُو يُردُه عَلَي البلَاد لَا مَال ولَا أَوْلَاد

What would bring him back to the country or town? He has neither property nor children.

Applied to one who has left a place and has no interest in it.

'Om. مُو stands for مَا = what.

299 مُو عَلَّمَك بِالقِسْمَة قَال بِمَا فِي وَجْه الذِيب

"What has taught thee (O fox,) to make a proper distribution?" It said, "What the wolf has (received) in its face."

Applied in the sense of taking a warning from the fate of others.

Origin.—It is based on a very old fable, in which a lion is supposed to have asked a wolf to distribute some meat between all the animals, and the latter having kept the best portion for itself, the lion was enraged and slapped it in the face. A fox having been next asked to do it, took for itself the worst part, whereupon the lion is supposed to have asked the fox the above question. Conf. story 101, Chap. I, "Nafhat-al-Yaman."

300 النَّار تَخَلَّف الرَّمَاد

Fire leaves (behind it) ashes.

Fire is here compared allegorically to a good and great man and ashes to a worthless son.

301 نَار السَمُر تَخَلَّف الجَمُر

The fire of the gum acacia tree leaves behind it cinders.

This proverb like the last one is also used allegorically, the cinders being compared to a son who is likely eventually to develop into a great man like his father.

302 النَّار مَا يُنْكَبّ عَلَيْهَا السُدِس

Fire cannot be put out with a *sidis* measure (*lit.* a *sidis* measure cannot be placed over fire). *Sidis* 'Om. = a wooden dry measure.

Eng. eq. Fire is not to be quenched with tow.

303 نَازِع وَلَا تُخِيب عَسَى يِلَك فِي النِّزَاعَة نَصِيب الْمَرَة وَلَّا الْحِمَارَة

Dispute and be not disappointed ; by disputing you will meet with luck—you will get either the woman or (at least) the she-ass.

Origin.—It seems to have originated from a very curious story. It is said that a man and his wife were one day on their way to another village, the woman riding a female donkey and the man walking by her side. On the road they met an old blind man, who was also proceeding in the same direction. They pitied him and asked him to ride the donkey. When they neared the place of destination, the owner of the donkey asked the old man to alight and go his own way, upon which the latter turning round said, that both the animal and the woman belonged to him and refused to give them up. The owner argued in vain with the old man, and the matter had eventually to be referred to the village authorities, who decided that either the woman or the donkey must belong to the old man. يِلَك stands for لَك and وَلَّا for وَإِلَّا

304 نَاقَة الْكَذَّاب رِزْمَانَة

The she-camel of a liar must tire (in the end). Conf. No. 114.

305 مُنَقَّاى مِن الصُّبَّة فَس فِي النَّضَد

Selected out of the heap it (a date) went bad in the bag. نَقَّى 'Om.=he selected. صُبَّة 'Om.=a heap of dates before they are packed. فَس 'Om.=it rotted dry so that it crumbled as a fine powder. نَضَد 'Om.=a heap of date bags arranged one over another with the object of draining off the treacle which oozes out of the dates.

Applied to a favourite thing or person not answering one's expectations.

306 وَا خَرَاب الدَّار إِذَا تَعَامَلُوا السَّنُّور وَالْفَار

Alas for the country when the cat and the rat join together in working !

Remedy worse than the disease.

This proverb seems to be based on the version of the destruction of the great *sadd* (dyke) of Márab in Yaman, given by al-Bagawee in his مَعَالِم التَّنْزِيل Conf. F. A. P., Caput I, No. 453.

307   تَوَدَّر بِنْهَا وتَرَبِّى غَبْنَهَا

She leaves off her (legitimate) child and brings up her bastard one.

Applied to a person who gives up a real claim and fights for an imaginary one.

Eng. eq. Catch not at the shadow and lose the substance.

308   وَلَّا فِيهَا وَلَّا فِي التِّبْن

Either it (the stick) will hit it (the ball) or fall in the straw.

A contest has only two ends ; one can either win or lose.

This proverb is based on a certain game of children in which the player has to hit a ball with a small stick.

309   وَيْش دَرَّى الحِمَار بِأَكَل الكُنَّار

What has taught the ass to eat jujubes ?

كُنَّار from P. =jujubes.   وَيْش stands for أَيْش

Eng. eq. To cast pearls before swine.

310   هَزَّة مِن المَزَّة وضَرْطَة مِن العَافِية

Shaking is the result of cheerfulness, and breaking wind with a sound is the result of good health.

Applied to one who is insolent or proud on account of wealth or any other cause.

311   هِي تَرْقَص ومِن عُمْرهَا يَنْقَص

She (a she-goat) dances, but her life-time is becoming shortened.

Applied to the unsuitableness of an action, dancing being an expression of joy, whilst life becoming shorter is a matter for sorrow or grief.

312   هَيْن بَغْلَة ضَاقَت بِدَقَلْهَا

What *bagleh* ever becomes straitened on account of its own mast ?

Bagleh=a kind of small sailing vessel. Conf. No. 249. هَيْن stands for أَيّة =what ?

313   يَا سَارِقُ الدِّيكَ فُوْقَ رَاسَكَ الرِّيش

O stealer of the cock, on your head is the feather.

Eng. eq. The guilty conscience is its own accuser.

314   يَا غَرِيب كُون اَدِيب

O stranger, be well-behaved.

Advice to a stranger in a foreign place.

315   يُوْم سِكُعْتُ كَلِنِي السَّمَك ويُوْم غَفَقْتُ كَلِنِي الطَّيْر

When I sink fish eat me and when I float birds eat me. سكع 'Om.
= it sank to the bottom. غَفَّ 'Om. = it floated.

In a dilemma. Conf. No. 274.

316   يُوْم الشَّرَاطَة مَا شَبْعَانْ لِيف

Even on the day of cleaning the date-palms, he is not satisfied with
their fibres.

Applied to a discontented man who is not satisfied even when he
has plenty.

شَرَاطَة 'Om. = the operation of pulling out the bottoms of date-
palm branches, which remain attached to the trunks after the
branches are broken off, with an iron instrument named مَنْخَلَب
During this operation a considerable quantity of the fibrous tissue
of palms is torn off and scattered about.

317   يُوْم يَطِيح شُوْب الكُنَّار ويَرَوَّح الكُعْك يَتَوَازَن لَيْل ونَهَار

When the jujube fruit falls and the cake of bread begins to smell,
night and day become equal. This happens in spring, when jujubes
becoming overripe fall off, and new wheat of which the cake of bread
is supposed to be made is collected, the smell of the cake evidently
referring to its being baked. يُوْم 'Om. = when.

318   يُوم مَا رَامَت عَلَى الجَرَاب دَارَت عَلَى الجِزْلَة

When she (a she-camel) could not carry a large bag of dates, she turned to a half one.

Every one must work according to his capacity.

رَام aor. يُرُوم ' Om. =he was able. جَرَاب a large mat bag containing preserved dates.

جِزْلَة ' Om. =half a *jaráb* or any piece cut off from a *jaráb*.

319   يُوم مَا عَرُفْت تَلْعَب قَالَت مَلْعَب ضَيِّق

When she did not know how to play, she said that the play-ground was narrow.

Eng. eq.   A bad workman quarrels with his tools.

320   يُوم النَّاس يُخَيِّطُو ثُوب السُّوَا يُحلِي أَنَا ضَرَبْت النَّكَارِير فِي

الجُونِية or فِي المَرْحَلَة

Whilst people sew *Suwáihilee cloth*, I have been braiding the edges of a gunny bag or a date basket.

Applied to inappropriateness of things, and also to one who wastes both a good thing and his time in trying to decorate a thing which is originally bad or ugly.

ثُوب السُّوَا يُحلِي ' Om. =a fine kind of long-cloth.

نَكَارِير ' Om. =a kind of braid made from two silk strings of different colours, generally sewn on to the neck or front of a shirt. جُونِية ' Om. =a gunny bag or sack. مَرْحَلَة ' Om. =a bag made of palm leaves,

ARABIA PAST AND PRESENT

OLEANDER MODERN POETS

OLEANDER LANGUAGE AND LITERATURE

OLEANDER TRAVEL BOOKS

THE AEOLIAN ISLANDS
Philip Ward

ALBANIA: A TRAVEL GUIDE
Philip Ward

BANGKOK: PORTRAIT OF A CITY
Philip Ward

COME WITH ME TO IRELAND
Philip Ward

JAPANESE CAPITALS: NARA, KYOTO, TOKYO
Philip Ward

ROSSYA: THE TRANS-SIBERIAN EXPRESS
Michael Pennington

TOURING CYPRUS
Philip Ward